MAD MEN®
The illustrated World

this book belongs to

....

meditations in an emergency

ICE CREAM

Menken's

MAD MEN®
The Illustrated World

WRITTEN & ILLUSTRATED BY

Dyna Moe

**BASED ON THE SERIES MAD MEN,
CREATED BY MATTHEW WEINER**

THE AUTHOR WOULD LIKE TO THANK:

WILL HiNES   DAN TELFER
JESSICA SARAH WILKES SILVIJA
STICKLES EDDIE MATT OZOLS
SUE GALLOWAY BRAWLEY CUTLER
"CHAMPAGNE" SPOONER

WEIDENFELD & NICOLSON

First published in Great Britain in 2010
by Weidenfeld & Nicolson

1 3 5 7 9 10 8 6 4 2

A CIP catalogue record for this book is available from the British Library.

ISBN: 978 0 297 86492 9

Printed in Italy

The Orion Publishing Group's policy is to use papers that are natural, renewable and recyclable and made from
wood grown in sustainable forests. The logging and manufacturing processes are expected to conform to
environmental regulations of the country of origin.

Art and Design by Dyna Moe

Weidenfeld & Nicolson

Orion Publishing Group Ltd
Orion House
5 Upper Saint Martin's Lane
London, WC2H 9EA

An Hachette UK Company

www.orionbooks.co.uk

CONTENTS

THE OFFICE • 6

THE HOME • 18

FASHION & BEAUTY • 40

ARTS & LEISURE • 48

MAINSTREAM & COUNTERCULTURE • 58

TRAVEL • 66

RAINY-DAY ACTIVITIES • 78

THE OFFICE

WHAT'S IN AN EXECUTIVE'S DESK

Bowl of marbles: There's nothing more relaxing.

Letter opener: A gift from personal friend J. Edgar Hoover.

Old trade papers: You'll get to them one of these days.

Ship in a bottle: To remind you that anything is possible if you put your mind to it.

Phone: So your secretary can let you know if you have a phone call.

Extra shirts: You never know when you might need to look extra crisp.

Clocks for every major global city: Will the boys in London be working late?

Stretchy forearm exercise machine: For relieving stress in the most intimidating way possible.

"I Love You, Daddy" valentine from the kids: Keep this around to trigger existential crises.

"To do" list: "Laundry, Read Trades, Campaign Pitch, Client's Wife."

Shoebox full of incriminating photos of your secret identity.

Loose cash: For any purchase you might not want to be traceable, or in case you suddenly run out of clean shirts.

Reading lamp.

Writing lamp.

'Rithmetic lamp.

Key to top-secret emergency drawer.

Drawer full of gadgets confiscated from underlings: Cap guns, chattering teeth, whoopee cushion, fireworks.

Casual tie.

Emergency extra-businessy tie.

Extra business cards.

Revolver: In case a client is very unsatisfied.

THINGS EVERY SECRETARY NEEDS TO KNOW

From *Miss Deaver's Secretarial School Manual* (1963)

A successful secretary enjoys the feeling of being indispensable to an important man. She realizes that a secretarial career calls for the utmost in loyalty, understanding, and—perhaps most important—tact. In fact, most of her time will be spent loyally making up for her employer's behavior with clients while tactfully avoiding his meaty hands and leering advances. The suggestions in this section will help you simplify daily office routines, become more efficient, and keep your trap shut.

THE SECRETARY AS STENOGRAPHER

The traditional shorthand system replaces words with letters or symbols. Here are some examples:

To Whom It May Concern:
I am writing to inform
you that our company
lacks the resources and
manpower to pay you.

We are moving to a new
building and shutting
down our Accounts
Payable department.
Just try and find us.
You won't be able to.
Because you are a sucker.
Neener neener.

Sincerely,
Harvey Pringsickle,
Executive Vice President

THE OFFICE MAIL

On your desk, you should have a box labeled "Incoming Mail" and a box labeled "Outgoing Mail." This is for appearances only, of course. In reality, you should have a complex system of pulleys and baskets set up in the space underneath your desk that will keep it hidden from view as you take each envelope, steam it open, read its contents, report any untoward content to your employer's supervisor, and save any personal items for potential blackmail or as insurance in case of firing. Select two letters at random to bring to your employer and shred the rest.

FILING

To get the most out of your filing system, it is absolutely necessary that you understand the underlying principles on which filing systems are built. Most files are built on a combination of principles, be they alphabetical, chronological, indexing, cross-indexing, color-coding, geographical, or Dewey. Remember: If someone can figure out your system, you can be replaced. So make it as complicated as possible.

OFFICE PRINTING

There are many modern options these days for the duplication of materials. These include stencil duplicating (the secretary creates a stencil with a safety razor blade and then has the stencil sent out to a professional company), photo-offset duplicators (a metal plate is made that can be used for thousands of copies), spirit duplicating (requires prayer), multigraphing (a special ribbon is inserted in the typewriter), photographic copying (used for photographs and multitone charts, the work is done by a photostat company), and varityping and automatic typewriters (a tape or master record of an original letter is made and then approximately 250 letters can be produced). With each of these options, you can get copies made in as little as a week. Isn't it amazing to live in the modern era!

SPECIAL TIP

The "tickler file" is the mainspring of efficiency in any office. It is, of course, a list of employees ranked by how susceptible they are to tickling. Employees are ranked on a "Fun Meter," from "Ol' Stony Face" to "Serious Squealer!!!" and then grouped accordingly at the Annual Office Pillow Fight.

CARE OF MONEY AND BANK ACCOUNTS

What word in the English language contains three sets of double letters in a row? Give up? The answer is "bookkeeping"! Now that you've learned this fun fact, try not to embezzle any money.

THE OFFICE BEAUTIFUL

When decorating, keep in mind the concept of primary and secondary colors. Suggested color schemes include:

- Chartreuse and yellow upholstery combined with brown carpeting.
- Olive green and beige upholstery, beige carpeting, one wall white and the others pale green, with white draperies. A desk of olive green with a white top would be effective in this office.
- Gold, orange, and yellow-beige upholstery with golden yellow vinyl flooring.

Try not to stray from these suggestions. You want your office to look timeless and modern, not the relic of a particular era that will eventually be captured in critically acclaimed television shows.

All incandescent lighting should be replaced with fluorescent lighting immediately. You may also wish to brick over any windows. The harsh flutter of fluorescents will make it easier to weed out easily distracted employees and epileptics.

Flowers and plants make lovely accents in any office. For limited budgets, artificial flowers are an attractive option. But don't let them become dust catchers! There is nothing more depressing than an artificial flower arrangement covered in dust. Nothing. Not even that time you cut yourself while staring into your own face in the mirror just to see if you could feel *anything*.

Office Emergency: Accidental Foot Amputation

Use boiling water to sterilize any and all cutting equipment. While you're up, remember to put a new pot on for the rest of the office. It's only decent.

Attempt to distract your patient with your best drinking story. Avoid references to your inability to walk properly or phrases like "put my foot in my mouth" or "stand on your own two feet."

Newspapers can soak up blood, but make sure everyone in the office had a chance to read it first. Use the Classifieds; nobody likes that.

Get the paper cutter from your art department. Humans are thicker than paper and it may take more than one try to remove mangled half-attached limbs. Keep at it!

Belts make excellent tourniquets. Borrow a belt from a coworker with well-sized pants to prevent any pants-dropping embarrassment.

(In a pinch, grab the most hideous necktie. You're doing that guy a favor on top of saving a life.)

Use the cheap liquor to sterilize the wound. Take a bottle from the office rummy and save the good stuff—everyone will need a glass after living through this.

BOB VS. ADVERTISING

"The real danger of the advertising man is that they are creating images," said Bob Newhart on his 1960 album *The Button-Down Mind of Bob Newhart*, before launching into a seven-minute dressing-down of the presidential elections and the influence of the advertising industry on candidates. According to Bob's routine, Lincoln was no longer a quirky and enigmatic assemblage of features, but a calculated series of choices (or lack thereof) being gently coaxed by a public relations director. The hat, the beard, even a leisurely night at the theater—all were imagined to have come from the slick and callous world of the men on Madison Avenue—smooth talkers who shaped our entire culture.

The first things Bob's imagined ad man had to say about the Wright Brothers: *Where will all the passengers fit? What about a toilet?* The fantastic achievement of flight was ignored in favor of the nitty-gritty of how they were going to sell it to a whining, irritable public.

Bob was an odd alternative to the Borscht Belt comics of his time. Lacking any kind of bravado, and often with minimal irony, he would set up a hypothetical situation, announce that it "might go a little something like this," and dive right into a character's voice. While he might first have come across as an unassuming office accountant, this bookish personality gave him the ability to parody the smartest men working: ad men.

Many of these routines were one-sided conversations where the other person's end of the dialogue was imagined, and Newhart would use the silence to ratchet up the awkwardness and tension. The technique came organically; he originally started doing comedy routines in 1958 over the phone with a partner he met in copywriting, and he recorded his skits as radio auditions. (This radio-friendly audio genesis is the reason his comedy albums remain so popular and influential today.)

The Button-Down Mind of Bob Newhart was an instant success. On the album charts, it crushed even Elvis Presley, whose stammer was also intentional, though perhaps delivered with a bit more swagger.

INVENTING THE OFFICE

The concept of "the office" as we know it is a relatively modern innovation. Back in the Victorian era, the average shop had a clerk to do simple bookkeeping, but a floor full of people at desks devoted solely to white-collar paper shuffling didn't come into its own until the turn of the twentieth century.

The office was modeled on the factory: rows and rows of identical desks of workers who plugged away at figures the way their downstairs equivalents plugged rivets into tractors or electric fans or whatever consumer goods they were mass-producing. The obsession was with "efficiency," squeezing as much work out of the day as possible, treating the workers as mechanical extensions of their adding machines. Talking during office hours was prohibited, as was leaving your desk, except at pre-approved break times.

One prominent writer on the subject was F. W. Taylor, who insisted there was only "one best way" to do any task and its use must be rigorously enforced on workers. How they felt about this was not his concern, as he considered his workers too stupid to understand what they were doing. He, as you might imagine, was not well liked by labor unions, but conversely, his scientific management writings had fans in both Hitler and Lenin.

A follower of Taylor, Frank Bunker Gilbreth Sr. used cutting-edge film and photo equipment to analyze efficiency in movement. One of his favorite experiments involved attaching lightbulbs to a secretary's hands as she collated paperwork. He studied the light arcs created in a long-exposed photograph as proof of "wasted movement" that needed to be corrected with more rules. (Gilbreth's need for efficiency trickled into his home life as well. His son, the fifth child out of twelve, wrote *Cheaper by the Dozen* about the Gilbreth family.)

Finally, in the 1950s, the novel idea was floated that a happy worker would be more productive. Although today fluorescent lights and dropped acoustic tile ceilings are symbolic of office depression, in the midcentury office space they were modern, clean, and allowed for central air-conditioning and heat. The office space had, for the first time, far better amenities than the homes of most of the workers.

In the 1950s, the Quickborner Team led by Eberhard and Wolfgang Schnelle created the idea of Bürolandschaft, or "office landscaping." Suddenly corporate headquarters sprouted potted plants and modern designer furniture arranged in organic groupings in an open-floor plan. Unfortunately, by the mid-1960s, the cubicle wall was invented to inject some privacy into the free-flowing office landscape. It was the beginning of the end.

THE SECRETARY'S ARSENAL

Telephone: Among its state-of-the-art features is a springy three-foot cord, scientifically engineered to maximize wrapping around your finger during boring calls.

Typewriter: Even if you have the best WPM in the office, no one will agree to call you "the QWERTY Cutie."

Desk lamp: Use a low-wattage bulb to give yourself a diffused, Greta Garbo–like glow; switch in a high-wattage bulb to interrogate suspects, police state–style.

File cabinet: Like a steel mausoleum within arm's reach, it's the place where press releases from three years ago go to die.

Carbon paper: More efficient than a monk scribe, but slightly messier.

Mechanical calculator: The height of arithmetic sophistication requires an intensive three-week certification course to operate.

Copier: Once people figured out they could use this to secretly copy their birthday party flyers, office sneakiness increased by 25 percent.

Rubber fingertips: Wear them while filing to avoid paper cuts. They double as earplugs when people laugh at how ridiculous you look wearing them.

Stapler: It's a stapler.

ART DEPARTMENT ACCOUTREMENTS

PROPORTIONAL SCALE

PERCENTAGE OF ORIGINAL SIZE

NUMBER OF TIMES OF REDUCTION

SIZE OF ORIGINAL

MAGIC MARKER
These early markers are expensive, dry out quickly, and reek of formaldehyde.

PROPORTION WHEEL
A quick spin tells you what scale to use to shoot the final art.

SOLV

TOXIC

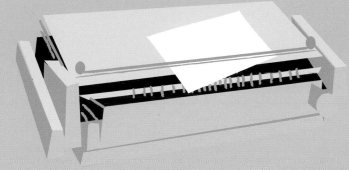

WAXER
An alternative to rubber cement for pasting up. Applies superheated molten wax in a thin layer over the back of artwork . . . and anything else caught in its rollers.

HABERULE
To calculate the vertical spacing between lines of type.

SOLVENT
To clean up all the wax and rubber cement you get everywhere. If you haven't passed out from being burned, the noxious smell of known carcinogens will finish you.

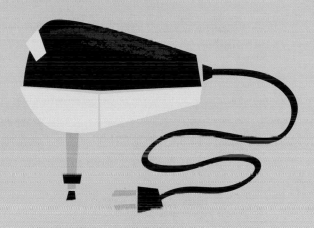

ELECTRIC ERASER
Used with metal "erasing shields," as the dental-drill motor inside has a habit of getting away from you and erasing through illustration board, desktops, human flesh . . .

TABORET
Because you gotta put it all somewhere.

NOVELTY FRENCH CURVE
No matter the level of technical sophistication, there's always room for crude sex humor.

DEALING WITH A DIFFICULT CLIENT

A difficult client can be almost as time-consuming and cranky as a newborn baby. The only difference is you can't breast-feed a client to make him feel better. Well, you could…but here are some other tips:

1. Set up a 24-hour phone line just for your difficult client. Include one direct extension to an employee dedicated exclusively to baking cinnamon rolls to accommodate your client's insatiable appetite. A well-fed client is a less disagreeable one.

2. Convince your client that you're a man of good, solid values to build confidence and trust. Stage impromptu family bible readings that your client can walk in on. Go with the Book of Job; after what he's put you through it should have particular resonance.

3. If he's rude on set, sleep with his wife.

4. A demanding client expects you to drop whatever it is you're doing (sleeping, eating, seducing a kindergarten teacher) and make yourself available for a meeting at all hours of the night. Plot out the easiest routes to get to your client. It may be helpful to build a pulley system that can lift you directly to your car. Every minute saved is another minute spent pleasing your client.

5. Liquid courage. Drink as many highballs as possible to get you through the day.

6. When your client is explaining something and using a phrase that could be interpreted as a double entendre, wait him out. Give him the benefit of the doubt that he's not talking about sex but about business instead. After you've made a deal, shaken on it, and your client has left, know that he was indeed making some sort of reference to sex and move along with your day.

7. Be stern, confident, and strong when speaking to your client. He will respect that. After a few moments of respect, he will chide you like you are a five-year-old boy and you respect that. See tip #4 to help make you more respecting.

8. Be like the son he never had. In fact, why not try actually fooling him into thinking you might be his son? Slightly alter your way of speaking, linger a bit in your handshakes to build a connection, forge some documents—you're already pretty good at that last one so it really should be a breeze.

9. If he wants the moon, get him the moon. Crazy can't be talked down from the moon.

10. If all else fails, try breast-feeding.

THE HOSPITABLE AMBITIONS OF CONRAD HILTON

Born in 1887 of Augustus Halvorson Hilton, Mary Genevieve Laufersweiler, and the harsh sands of New Mexico, Conrad Hilton was grit and elegance at once. His family was large, and he was determined to make his name at a young age. Though he was offered a job at a hotel his father purchased, he found this entry-level position too confining for his personality. In the 1910s, he served both as a senator and in the army.

Whereas a pedestrian entrepreneur looks to make money from nothing, Conrad had foreseen the ultimate bounty of war. And he realized that domination is not about politics; rather, it's about civilizations across the map bearing your name. Conrad scrambled to find investment capital from as many legitimate sources as possible until no project seemed too extravagant for his budget. The Dallas Hilton, built in 1925, cost a monocle-popping $1,360,000 to build and still stands today. But when the Great Depression hit, he was no less skilled at tightening his belt.

The moment the Depression began to wane, his empire unfurled its mighty tentacles once again, and he helped lead the economy back into recovery. Vacant floors of underperforming locations were closed. Guest rooms were spared phone lines. And after a few years of pinching pennies, he was able to purchase back every asset he lost. Setting down firm roots in his home state as well as Texas, Hilton hotels sprang up like victory gardens across the United States. Fifty-four locations opened overseas. And after grappling with its owners for what seemed an eternity, Conrad bought New York's infamous Waldorf as a crowning post-war achievement.

But success did not make him docile or complacent. He received six honorary degrees and penned his autobiography at the height of his success. An imposing, energetic man, he was known to keep fit and hit the golf courses not only in middle age but well into his nineties. Beautiful starlets paved the way to a more settled and serene family life, and his third wife proved to be his most beloved. He died a happily married billionaire, his legacy an unstoppable force that continues well into the twenty-first century.

THE HOME

Your Commute

Everywhere we look, mankind asserts its dominance over nature. And what display of industry is more comforting than a steel train carrying you from your downtown office to your quiet suburban home?

Grand Central Terminal—As you settle into your seat, be mindful not to lock eyes with any strangers. One of them may be a bunkmate from Korea, primed to unravel your true identity. Well, if you're Don, it's a quantifiable risk.

University Heights—Heading out of Manhattan and through the outer borough of the Bronx, it might be a good time to head to the bar car and order a Gibson martini for the ride so you can erase the image of the secretary burned into your retinas.

Yonkers—Your newspaper may start to get boring at this point in the commute. Of course, if you're a big-time ad exec, this might also be where your mistress, Suzanne, slides into the seat next to you.

Tarrytown—The town where Don's third child, Eugene Scott Draper, was born. Once a year, late at night, you might see Don Draper at the train crossing adjacent to the station, slumped over his steering wheel drunk while trying to dodge his eldest son's birthday party.

Ossining—The station Don exits, when he feels like heading home.

Peekskill—Did Don just intimidate you into leaving your father's Lincoln in his driveway? Not to worry, your home in Peekskill is just a short and humiliating train ride away.

Poughkeepsie—Having a flashback of your stepmother and half brother crying outside the train car window? Wake up! You've napped too long and are in Poughkeepsie.

NEWLYWEDS' SUPPER FOR TWO

Every young housewife gets a thrill seeing her workingman's weary face light up at the prospect of a lovingly prepared home-cooked meal after a long day at the office.

Lettuce Wedge with Blue Cheese Dressing

½ cup white vinegar · 1½ cups vegetable or canola oil · 1½ tsp salt · 2 tsp sugar · 1 thin slice of onion · ½ tsp paprika (optional) · ½ tsp dry mustard · ¼ lb blue cheese · ½ head iceberg lettuce

In a blender, puree vinegar, oil, salt, sugar, onion, and spices until smooth. Add crumbled blue cheese and pulse until it's the consistency you want, lumpy or smooth. Cut lettuce head half into two even wedges. Serve each wedge on a salad plate, drizzled with blue cheese dressing.

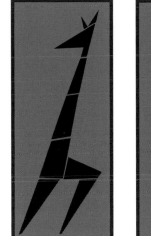

· ·

Steak Diane

3 Tbsp butter · 2 (10-oz) sirloin steaks · 2 Tbsp cognac · 4 Tbsp sherry · 2 Tbsp unsalted sweet butter · Chopped chives, to garnish · Salt and pepper, to taste

Cook steaks one at a time. Heat half the butter in a large frying pan. Add one steak, fry on each side to taste. Pour on half the cognac and set on fire. Douse the flambé with half the sherry, then turn off heat, transfer to serving plate, pat with half the sweet butter, and sprinkle with chives, salt, and pepper. Repeat with the second steak.

Tip: *Wait until your husband's home before you start frying the steaks. You don't want the succulent sauce to congeal! On the other hand, you don't want to make your hungry man wait for his dinner. Work fast.*

· ·

Peas with Bacon

½ medium onion, chopped · 1 Tbsp butter · 2 slices of bacon, chopped · 1 (16-oz) can peas, drained · Salt and pepper, to taste

Sauté onions in butter until soft. Add bacon, continue sautéing until browned. Add peas. Continue cooking until heated through.

Parker House Rolls

Buy a bag of frozen rolls at the supermarket and follow the heating directions on the bag. Your kitchen is not a bakery, and you're a busy girl.

· ·

Aunt Alice's Lemon Luscious

1 package lemon-flavored gelatin dessert (e.g., Jell-O) · 1 container frozen whipped topping (e.g., Cool Whip), thawed

Make lemon gelatin as directed on the box, but cut setting time in half. Use a deep dish or bowl, with plenty of room above the gel line. When half set, whisk half the whipped topping into the gelatin until the stuff has an even consistency and is a fluffy, opaque yellow cream. Smooth the surface, or pour the whole concoction into a fresh mold. Set for another hour or more, and serve with dinner as a side, or as a dessert, garnished with remaining whipped topping.

PLANTER'S PUNCH

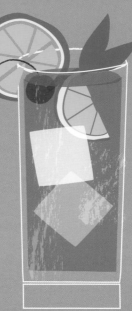

2 oz orange juice
2 oz pineapple juice
2 oz lime juice (sweetened)
1¼ oz white rum
1¼ oz amber rum
1¼ oz Jamaican rum
1 tsp grenadine

Combine juices and rums in a shaker. Shake well, and strain over ice. Top with grenadine.

MINT JULEP

4 cups water
2 cups sugar
4 cups fresh mint leaves, chopped
4 cups bourbon

Combine water and sugar in a medium saucepan; bring to a boil. Reduce heat to medium and cook for 10 minutes. Reduce heat to low, add chopped mint leaves and simmer 30 minutes. Let syrup stand at room temperature overnight. Strain. Fill julep cups with crushed ice. Combine bourbon and mint syrup; pour over ice. Garnish with extra mint.

WHISKEY SOUR

1½ oz whiskey
4 oz sour mix (recipe follows)
1 maraschino cherry

Combine the whiskey and sour mix in a large old-fashioned glass with crushed ice. Stir, add the cherry, and serve.

Sour Mix
1 oz lemon juice
1 oz sugar
2 oz water

Combine lemon juice and sugar, then dilute with water and stir to dissolve sugar.

FROZEN DAIQUIRI

1½ oz light rum
1 Tbsp triple sec
1½ oz lime juice
1 tsp sugar
1 cup crushed ice
1 maraschino cherry

Combine all ingredients (except for the cherry) in an electric blender and blend at a low speed for 5 seconds, then blend at a high speed until firm. Top with the cherry and serve.

PINK LADY

1½ oz gin
1 tsp grenadine
1 tsp light cream
1 egg white

Combine in a shaker with ice. Shake well, then strain into a cocktail glass and serve.

CUBA LIBRE

¾ oz lime juice
2 oz rum (white)
5 oz cola

Put lime juice and a twist of lime into highball glass. Add rum and fill with cola.

BLOODY MARY

1 oz vodka
3 oz tomato juice
Dash celery salt
Dash ground black pepper
Dash Tabasco
2–4 dashes Worcestershire
⅛ tsp horseradish
Dash lemon or lime juice

Pour vodka into a highball glass filled with ice. Fill with tomato juice and add remaining ingredients. Garnish with a celery stalk.

VODKA GIMLET

2 oz vodka
½ oz lime juice

Combine in a shaker with ice. Shake well, then strain into a chilled cocktail glass. Serve with a squeeze of lime.

FORMAL SIT-DOWN DINNER

Get out the good china and make sure the furniture is dusted, the children are invisible, and the imported European beer is ice-cold. You are the shadow partner in your husband's success when he has important clients and their wives over for an elegant home-cooked meal, so remember, appearance is everything and too much flavor can offend; serve something beautiful and bland.

Broiled Lamb Chops

So elegant, but so easy to scale up or down depending on how many last-minute guests your husband adds without warning.

½- to ¾-inch cut lamb shoulder chops (1 per person) · Italian herb mix or dry salad dressing mix · 2–3 tomatoes, sliced

Cut several vertical slashes through the fat on the edge of each chop. Place the chops on a broiler pan, and brush the tops with the herbs, mixed with a little olive oil. Broil chops for 8–10 minutes, take them out, turn them over, brush the bottoms with the herb mix, and broil for 4 minutes more. Serve on a platter, garnished with tomato slices.

Garden Jewels Loaf

This, technically, is a salad. Gelatin makes it a salad to impress.

2 packages unflavored gelatin (e.g., Jell-O) · 3½ cups hot water · ¼ cup sugar · ½ tsp salt · 1 Tbsp vinegar · 2 Tbsp lemon juice · 1 cup cauliflower, broken into small florets and cooked · ½ cup carrots, sliced and cooked · ¼ cup celery, diced · ¼ cup radishes, sliced · ¼ cup green onions or chives, chopped · 9–12 whole green beans or asparagus spears · 3–4 strips of pimiento or roasted red pepper

Dissolve gelatin in hot water, and mix in sugar, salt, vinegar, and lemon juice. Pour ½ inch of gelatin mix into an 8-inch loaf pan; chill until set. Meanwhile, toss the cauliflower, carrots, celery, radishes, and green onions in the remaining warm gelatin; set aside. When the ½ inch layer of gelatin is set, carefully place green beans or asparagus and pimiento on top, arranged in an attractive pattern. Gently pour the vegetable-gelatin mix over the green beans, and chill until set. Arrange lettuce and parsley on a serving plate, and tap out the gelatin loaf onto the plate to serve.

Rice Ring

Ring molds give strength and stability to unorganized rice, showing you demand the most from your starches.

1 cup medium-grain white rice · ½ tsp ground nutmeg · ¾ cup almonds or pecans, chopped · ¼ cup melted butter · 1 Tbsp parsley, chopped · Salt and pepper, to taste · 1 can mushrooms, sliced or quartered · 2 cans cream of anything soup

Cook rice according to directions, if from a box, or in 2 cups of boiling water, covered, for 25–30 minutes. Transfer rice to a mixing bowl, and stir in nutmeg and almonds. Pack rice firmly into a 7-inch ring mold, then pour melted butter into rice. Place the mold in a pan of hot water, and bake it at 350 degrees for 20 minutes. Once cool enough to handle, loosen the edges of the mold with a knife, and turn rice ring out on a plate. Sprinkle with chopped parsley and salt and pepper, if you like, and fill the ring with cream soup and mushrooms, heated separately.

Pink Dream

Like the Garden Jewels Loaf, this frozen tube is also a "salad," but go ahead and serve it as a dessert. Everyone will be too full by then, anyway.

6 oz cream cheese, softened to room temperature · 1 cup mayonnaise · 1 (15-oz) can fruit cocktail, drained · ½ cup maraschino cherries, drained and quartered · 2½ cups miniature marshmallows, or 24 large marshmallows, chopped · 1 cup whipped cream or non-dairy whipped topping (e.g., Cool Whip) · Red food coloring or reserved maraschino cherry juice

In a large mixing bowl, blend together cream cheese and mayo. Add fruits and marshmallows and stir. While stirring, add a few drops of food coloring or a couple teaspoons of maraschino juice, until the mixture is the desired pink hue. Pour mixture into two 1-quart round, rinsed ice cream containers, or two cleaned coffee cans. Cover with plastic wrap, and place in the freezer for at least 6 hours. Before serving, take tubes out of the freezer and rest a few minutes, then tap out onto serving tray, cut into slices, and garnish with extra fruit.

SCREW DRIVER

2 oz vodka
5 oz orange juice

Mix in a highball glass with ice. Garnish with a slice of orange.

MAI TAI

1 oz gold rum
1 oz dark rum
1 oz triple sec
½ oz lime juice
½ oz orgeat syrup

Combine all ingredients in a shaker. Shake well, then strain over crushed ice. Garnish with fruits and mint.

HOT TODDY

1 oz brandy
1 oz honey
½ lemon slice

Combine in a mug or punch cup, and add hot water to fill. Stir with a cinnamon stick, if desired.

SIDECAR

1 oz Cointreau
1 oz lemon juice
1 oz cognac

Combine in a shaker with cracked ice. Shake well, then strain into a chilled cocktail glass with a sugared rim.

TOM COLLINS

2 oz London dry gin
1 tsp superfine sugar
½ oz lemon juice
Club soda

Combine gin, sugar, and juice in a highball glass mostly full of cracked ice. Stir briefly, top with club soda.

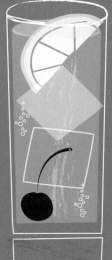

SEVEN AND SEVEN

1½ oz Seagram's 7
4½ oz 7UP

Combine in a highball glass on the rocks. Mix and serve.

"THE USUAL, MOMMY?"

BRANDY ALEXANDER

1 oz brandy
1 oz crème de cacao
1 oz heavy cream

Combine in a shaker with cracked ice. Shake well, then strain into a chilled cocktail glass.

SLOE GIN FIZZ

1 oz sloe gin
¾ oz lemon juice
1 oz simple syrup
Club soda

Combine gin, juice, and syrup in a shaker with cracked ice. Shake well, then strain into a chilled glass. Top with soda and serve.

MANHATTAN

2 oz rye whisky
1 oz Italian vermouth
2 dashes Angostura bitters

Combine in a shaker with cracked ice. Shake well, then strain into a chilled cocktail glass and garnish with a maraschino cherry.

the Bachelor's buffet

A modern, sophisticated man knows cooking isn't just for the girls. He demands excellent taste in his cognac, his LPs, his surroundings, and, yes, his food as well. To show off and share a truly international spread with friends compliments *your* good taste for choosing it and *theirs* for choosing you as their party host.

Deviled Ham Dip

Smooth and pink, with a devilish kick of horseradish. A fantastic opening to any buffet.

1 (6-oz) can deviled ham · 2 hard-boiled eggs, chopped · 1 tsp horseradish · 2 Tbsp dill relish · 1 Tbsp milk

Puree all ingredients in a blender until smooth. If you're artistically minded, omit the milk and sculpt the spread into an elegant, asymmetrical, abstract shape, or a reclining nude. Serve with crudités.

. . . .

Rumaki

A classic hors d'oeuvre with an ambiguously exotic kick. Also a great starter for a fancy dinner party.

1 lb chicken livers · Soy sauce · 1 small can water chestnuts, sliced · Port wine · Bacon

Wash the livers and place them in a glass bowl. Sprinkle on a few dashes of soy sauce, and allow livers to marinate. Drain canned water chestnuts and marinate them in port wine to cover, 10–20 minutes. Cut the bacon into ½- to 1-inch slices. Take a piece of liver and a water chestnut slice and wrap them together in a piece of bacon. Secure with a wooden toothpick, or place several rumaki on a metal skewer. Place rumaki in the broiler and broil until bacon is crisp and set. Serve with toothpicks.

Swedish Meatballs

Ah, the Swedes. Clean-lined furniture, depressing cinema, beautiful women…and delicious meatballs.

5 Tbsp butter or margarine · 3 Tbsp finely chopped onion · ¾ cup light cream · ¾ cup packaged dry breadcrumbs · 1½ lb ground chuck · ½ lb ground pork · 2 eggs, lightly beaten · 2 Tbsp salt · ¼ tsp pepper · ¼ tsp allspice · ½ tsp cloves

Heat 1 tablespoon butter in skillet and sauté onion 3 minutes, or until golden.

In large bowl, combine cream, ¾ cup water, and breadcrumbs. Add onion, ground meats, eggs, salt, pepper, allspice, and cloves; toss lightly to mix well. With a teaspoon, shape into 75 meatballs, about ¾ inch in diameter.

Heat 2 tablespoons butter in the same skillet, and sauté meatballs, a few at a time, until browned on all sides. Add more butter as needed. Remove meatballs, and set aside.

Sauce
2 Tbsp flour · ½ cup light cream · 1 tsp salt · Pepper, to taste

To make the sauce: Remove all but 2 tablespoons drippings from skillet. Stir in flour until smooth. Gradually stir in cream and 1½ cups water; bring to a boil, while stirring. Add salt and pepper.

Add meatballs. Heat gently for 5 minutes, or until heated through. Garnish with parsley and serve with toothpicks for ease of noshing.

2nd Avenue Blintzes

No woman can resist the siren song of "Do you like Ukrainian food?"

Cheese Filling
1 lb ricotta cheese · 4 oz cream cheese · 2 Tbsp butter, softened · ⅓ cup sugar

Batter
2 eggs · ½ tsp salt · 1 cup flour · 1 cup water

To make the filling: Combine all ingredients until smooth, and set aside.

To make the crepes: Beat the eggs, then add salt and flour until smooth. Gradually beat in water. Heat a cast-iron skillet and grease lightly with butter. Using a ladle or a ¼ cup, pour a measure of the batter into the skillet, and tilt the skillet quickly to spread. Once the crepe is dry on top, flip the crepe onto a plate (do not flip to fry the other side). Repeat until all batter is used.

To fold the blintzes: Place a crepe fried side up on a clean surface. Place 2 tablespoons of filling in the middle of the crepe, and fold into rectangles, covering the filling completely.

Once all blintzes are folded, reheat the skillet with a little more butter, and fry each blintz, flipping to brown each side. Serve with sour cream, apple sauce, or strawberry jam.

. . . .

'Ula'ula Polynesian Spareribs

A taste of the South Seas shows you're an academic and an adventurer. Thor Heyerdahl meets Margaret Mead.

3 lb pork spareribs · 3 Tbsp brown sugar · ¾ tsp salt · ½ cup soy sauce · ½ cup ketchup · 1 tsp ground ginger · Extra brown sugar and salt for rubbing

Rub ribs with brown sugar and salt—use smoked salt if you have it—and let stand for two hours. Meanwhile, combine remaining ingredients to make the sauce. Brush ribs with sauce, and let stand for another hour. Bake in the oven at 350 degrees for about 45 minutes or until ribs are tender, basting with sauce occasionally. Serve with remaining sauce, or make more to dip.

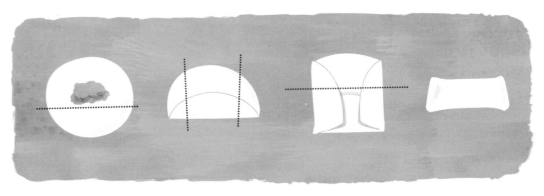

ELECTION Night Office PARTY

It's Joe Sr.'s golden boy versus the guy who put Alger Hiss in jail, by way of some microfilm hidden in a pumpkin patch. It's the New Frontier versus the Checkers speech. It's a Quaker (gasp!) versus a Catholic (GASP!!)! It's the 1960 presidential election, when America has to choose between two young, politically experienced Navy men.

What better way to wait out the results—which, thanks to the recent membership of Alaska and Hawaii to the electoral college, might take until 1 a.m. in New York—than an office party with your coworkers? For this occasion, there should be snacks, but the key part of this party is the drinks. You've already voted, you're excited about the future, and it's time to get slozzled.

SNACKS

Vienna Sausages with Dipping Sauce

For when you're too drunk to care what you put in your mouth.

1 cup red currant jelly · 1 cup yellow mustard · 2 (5-oz) cans Vienna sausages

In a saucepan on low heat, stir together jelly and mustard until the mix is a smooth consistency. It's your choice to heat the sausages or serve cold, but always serve dipping sauce warm.

. . . .

Avocado Dip

Not to be confused with guacamole! This is a patriotic, all-American condiment. Serve with plain potato chips, carrots, and celery.

1 ripe avocado · 3 Tbsp mayonnaise · 1 Tbsp lemon juice · ½ tsp salt · ½ tsp pepper

Puree all ingredients in a blender until smooth. Resist your temptation to add more flavorings.

DRINKS

Whether your candidate wins or loses, you'll need some stiff ones to get you through the night. By the time Alaska and Hawaii are called, you should already be upchucking in red, white, and blue. Since you don't have to do the cleaning up, why not bring a blender to the office party? These blender drinks are perfect for November 8, 1960.

El Presidente

2 jiggers rum · 1 jigger dry vermouth · 1 tsp grenadine · 1 cup cracked ice

Blend all ingredients, pour in a martini or daiquiri glass, and garnish with a cherry or orange peel.

. . . .

The Tricky Dick (aka Orange Velvet)

½ cup California white port · ½ cup California orange juice · 1 tsp lemon juice · 1½ cups cracked ice

Blend all ingredients, pour into a tall glass, and toast the man from Orange County and his dog, Checkers.

. . . .

Rose's Jack (aka Jack Rose)

1 oz lime juice · 2 jiggers New England apple brandy · 2 tsp grenadine · 1 egg white · ½ cup cracked ice

Blend all ingredients, pour, and drink. If you know any dead voters in Chicago, or fictional ones in Texas, pour yourself another.

. . . .

For your teetotalling third-partiers…

The Orval Faubus (aka Strawberry Soda)

⅓ cup frozen strawberries · 1 scoop vanilla or strawberry ice cream · 3 Tbsp milk · Sparkling water

Blend strawberries, ice cream, and milk for 20 seconds or until strawberries are pureed. Pour into a glass, leaving 1–2 inches from the rim, and top off with sparkling water. While drinking this at the office party, stand alone in a corner and grumble about Little Rock and desegregation.
(Author's note: Please don't actually do this.)

Finally…

The Results Are In (aka Between the Sheets)

1 jigger gin · 1 jigger brandy · 1 jigger Cointreau · 1 jigger lemon juice · 1 cup cracked ice

Blend all ingredients together for 5 seconds. Pour into whatever receptacle is still clean at 2 a.m., and try not to spill it on the boss's couch.

FAMILY PICNIC

Of course, you could go with peanut butter and jelly, but why not make your family picnic memorable, and not just for the squirrels that eat your left-behind garbage?

These three sandwich spreads can all be made in a blender, and go well with watercress, cucumber slices, and extra mayo. Serve on white bread with the crusts cut off, unless you're some kind of troublemaker.

Baked Bean Spread

1 cup canned baked beans
1 dill pickle, chopped
2 Tbsp mayonnaise

Puree all ingredients in the blender until smooth. Makes about 1 cup.

Deviled Ham and Cheese Spread with Sherry

The sherry can be omitted, but why would you do that?

8 oz cream cheese
1 (3-oz) can deviled ham
1 slice white onion
2 Tbsp sweet relish
¼ cup sherry
1 tsp Worcestershire
¼ tsp dry mustard
¼ tsp garlic powder
¼ tsp salt

Puree all ingredients in the blender until smooth. Makes about 1 ½ cups.

Walnut, Green Pepper, and Cheese Spread

1 green bell pepper, diced
½ cup walnuts
8 oz cream cheese, diced
¼ cup light cream
Dash salt and pepper
Dash Worcestershire

Puree all ingredients in the blender until peppers and walnuts are in small pieces. Makes about 1 ¼ cups.

DECORATING FOR THE HATED IN-LAW

In a perfect world, the family we acquire while reciting our nuptials would be conjured from the same heaven as our loving spouse.

But, of course, this is never the case. To love one's spouse most often means regarding them as Persephone, and your new in-laws as the acolytes of Hades, who desperately cling to her during those winter holidays.

Subtly show your in-laws your true feelings when outfitting the spare room in your otherwise heavenly home into a little corner of the underworld:

- An oil painting of ducks flying over a pond, begging to be fired upon by a rifle that does not exist. A handy reminder of the impotence that arrives with old age.

- An old army cot, to remind them that the one skill they retained from their years in the armed services is being able to sleep in sobering discomfort.

- Stationery sans pencil, because some suggestions are best in theory.

- Cedar panel walls maintain that authentic "this used to be a linen closet" look. (Also keeps moths from eating their cloth-like aged skin.)

- Vintage cotton sheets, the same pattern as last year's dining room curtains.

- Amber-tinted drinking glasses, so it always feels like someone's poured you a drink, even when they haven't and weren't planning on it anytime soon.

- A copy of *The Decline and Fall of the Roman Empire*, because warriors deserve to remember when they were fertile. And what sterilized them.

THE PERFECT OLD-FASHIONED

Sometime around 1880 at the Pendennis Club in Louisville, Kentucky, the old-fashioned was born. Some even say it was the first drink ever to be branded a "cocktail." True or not, it embodies all a cocktail should be—a golden ratio of spirit, sweet, bitter, sour, and water.

1 sugar cube
2 shakes Angostura bitters
2 orange slices
1 maraschino cherry
Rye whiskey*
Ice

Place the sugar cube in the bottom of a tumbler. Pour bitters over the cube. Add 1 orange slice and muddle.

Fill a short tumbler—called, appropriately enough, an "old-fashioned glass"—with ice, then fill to ½ inch from the rim with rye.

Add the cherry and the second orange slice to the rim.

Note: Seltzer or plain water is often used to top off this drink, but traditional bartenders do not approve of this method.

*Mr. Draper drinks rye, but the old-fashioned can be made with any number of whiskeys for a different flavor. In parts of the Midwest, using brandy is also popular.

a word on ice

Use clear, clean ice made from purified water free from the unwelcome oniony or fishy flavors of an overstuffed freezer.

muddler

Muddling is the action of pressing and mixing ingredients at the bottom of the glass. It can be done with the back of a spoon or with the specialized bar tool called a "muddler" (a kind of thin, bowling-pin-shaped pestle).

HANGOVER REMEDIES

A long night of hard emotional truths and hard alcohol takes its toll on a pretty face. Get back on your game and back to the housework with these simple pick-me-ups.

Fizzy Bull

1 can beef broth, cold
½ cup soda water
Squeeze of lemon

Stir together and serve on ice.

The Eye Opener

3 cups tomato or mixed vegetable juice
   (e.g., V8)
1–2 dashes Worcestershire
1–2 dashes hot sauce
1 small clove garlic

Puree all ingredients in a blender. Serve on ice.

Satan's Daiquiri

3 cups vegetable juice (e.g., V8)
1 scoop lime sherbet
4 tsp lemon juice
Dash of cinnamon

Puree all ingredients in a blender. Drink. Vow never to touch alcohol again.

The Prairie Oyster (Traditional)

A classic. Every hotel barkeep knows this one.

1 raw egg
1–2 dashes Worchestershire sauce
1–2 dashes hot sauce

Crack the egg into a shot glass. Add the sauces. Down the hatch!

The Ritz Cure

½ glass milk
1 bottle cola

Pour the milk. Shake the cola and pour it into the milk. Drink.

DIVORCE, AMERICAN-STYLE

What do you do if you want a divorce and your partner doesn't?

If you're well-heeled enough to drop everything for six weeks to establish residency, you move to Reno for a "quickie divorce." A favorite of the millionaire and movie star set back to the days of Mary Pickford and Cornelius Vanderbilt Jr., taking "the cure" or "getting Reno-vated" is a major industry for Nevada's Biggest Little City. A six-week stay on a resort-like "divorce ranch" and the traditional throwing of the wedding rings into the Truckee River from Virginia Street's "Bridge of Sighs" and the gay divorcé(e) is back on the market.

What if both parties want out of the marriage but there isn't any proof of wrongdoing?

You put on a show.

New York recognizes adultery as the only breach of a marriage contract and that adultery must be witnessed by a third party and presented as evidence. Try a private detective/mistress-for-hire team. They provide the girl, document the whole thing with a camera hiding in the bushes, and present it all to your lawyers in a neat little manila envelope…for a fee, of course.

GOVERNOR ROCKY

Nelson Aldrich Rockefeller (1908–1979)

Scion of a renowned industrialist family, political insider in Washington and New York, patron of the arts, developer of Rockefeller Plaza and other iconic buildings, philanthropist, governor of New York State—Nelson "Rocky" Rockefeller was *the* man about town by 1960. He and his wife, Mary Todhunter "Tod" Clark Rockefeller, appeared on the A-list of all the high-rolling parties in Gotham City.

Through his illustrious life and career, Rocky never seemed to rest. From raising rabbits as a young boy to working at his father's company's research laboratories to forging U.S.–Latin American trade and security policy under FDR to directing the Museum of Modern Art to overseeing art installments at "30 Rock," Nelson Rockefeller defined both industriousness with a small *i* and Industry with a capital *I*. In 1958, just a few years after leaving the Eisenhower administration, he was elected governor of New York. In 1960, he threw his name into the hat to challenge Vice President Richard Nixon as the GOP's presidential candidate. His party liked Nixon, though, and Rocky moved on to shaping the future of the Empire State through four terms in Albany—though he vied again for the presidential nomination in 1964, losing to Barry Goldwater, and in 1968, losing again to Nixon.

In 1961–62, Rocky's lifelong headline-making took a tabloid turn, as his marriage to Tod crumbled; his youngest son, Michael, an anthropologist, disappeared during an art-gathering expedition in New Guinea and was presumed dead; and Rocky's dalliances with other women came to light, including his affair with Margaretta Fitler* "Happy" Murphy, a divorcée, whom he married in 1963.

Nelson Rockefeller would go on to further national attention during the Attica prison riots in 1971, when as governor he ignored the inmates' request to negotiate with him and ordered state troopers to crush the insurgency, leaving 39 people dead. In 1974, he got as close as he ever would be to the presidency, when his old rival Nixon resigned and Gerald Ford appointed Rockefeller his new vice president. After leaving public office in 1977, Rocky dedicated his retirement to his great passion—modern art—and was rumored to have died at his desk while working on a book about his own collection.

* Yes, Fitler.

DECORATING AROUND AN OVERSIZED VICTORIAN FAINTING COUCH

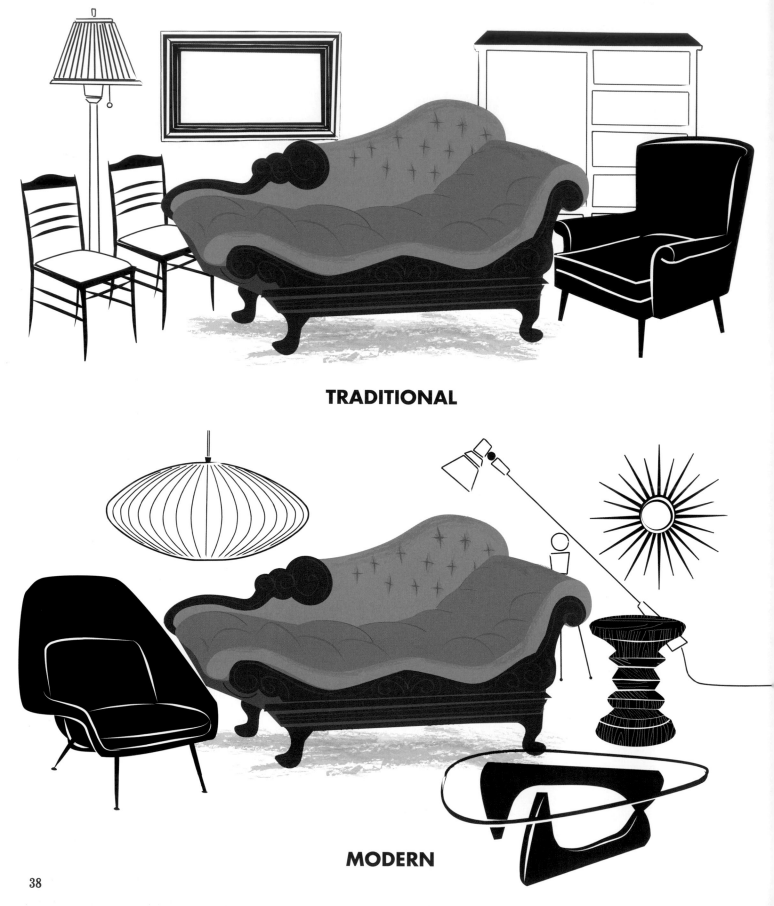

TRADITIONAL

MODERN

BRYAN BATT
and his fabulous sofa

When my partner, Tom, and I temporarily relocated to my hometown of New Orleans to open our fine gift/home furnishings shop, Hazelnut, we briefly stayed with my mother. Although we adore and love her to bits, a grown man of a certain age cannot reside for more than a week, maybe two, with his mom, and that goes double for his partner. There were no fits or fights, just the basic mental anguish of uncontrollably reverting to an emotional teenager, similar to when I last lived under the same roof. Luckily we were able to rent a fabulous carriage house just off St. Charles Avenue, home to the streetcar's hum and the Mardi Gras parade festivities once a year. Although we maintained our apartment in Manhattan, we really needed to be down South for the shop, unless I was called for a Broadway show, or, even better, a hit TV series. So the idea was born to take this more rustic place, with the original brick floors, and give it a more metropolitan feel. The living area was expansive, but our budget was restrictive, so I did my usual scouring of consignment shops and thrift stores. Being a New York actor for years, I was used to the high life when on Broadway, and the more inventive when off-Broadway.

While taking a stroll through the Salvation Army thrift store on Jefferson Highway in a neighboring suburb, I came across the perfect midcentury modern sofa. I imagined if it were reupholstered in a really great fabric other than the thread-worn hideous teal floral brocade, it could be way cool. So I laid down the $200, found a discount designer fabric store, and bought 18 yards of chocolate brown microfiber ultra suede, dropped it off at Aguilar's Upholstery, and my *Dick Van Dyke Show*, midcentury sofa was born...and I love it!

One of the definitive aspects of midcentury modern design is the shape, and this sofa has got it going on. The seating, seen especially in sofas of that period, is so different from the big plushy leather baseball glove loungers and rigid boxy-shaped couches of recent decades. In the 1950s and '60s, the look was very streamlined and lower to the ground. This design feature may have emerged due to the fact that homes built in that period tended to have lower ceilings, but that's just a guess. This sofa has a wonderful bowed or crescent arch to its form, and it inherently creates movement in the room, rather than just taking up space, sitting stagnantly against the wall. Another great feature, due to its shape, is the fact that in a large space the sofa could float in the middle, and due to its height, not divide the room. I recently moved to a new home with very high ceilings and for a moment was considering getting a new sofa, but she actually looks just perfect in the new space as well, proving that good design is timeless.

—Bryan Batt

FASHION & BEAUTY

WHAT DOES YOUR SECRETARY'S HAIR SAY ABOUT HER?

"My brain has been eaten by the mutant spiders inside my hair."

"I'm all the drama of Maria Callas in a Pat Nixon package."

"I only have sexual fantasies about my husband and my pastor."

"My hair is as one-sided as my thoughts on civil rights."

"I am a child, please treat me as one."

"Goo whiz, isn't Mary Martin just the absolute most!"

"Someone moved my cup of pencils a half inch to the left and I am about to explode."

"Actually, I prefer the term 'spinster.'"

"I never pay full price, even for dental work."

"The higher the hair, the closer to God."

"Gosh, I'd like to go to a booze-soaked gin joint!"

"I am a booze-soaked gin joint."

"I've been forwarding all your mail to HUAC."

"*New York Herald Tribune!*"

"Get me a Pall Mall, mister, 'cause I'm about to take your job."

"What *is* the mystery of the old clock?"

VIVA BOUFFANT!

Born the toast of high society on the runways of Paris's finest couturiers, and adding visual contrast to the sack dress, the bouffant took the halls of power atop the head of the First Lady and went Hollywood on Holly Go-Lightly. Then, it became a trickle-down populist on the heads of office girls and trophy wives . . . gaining new height as it mutated into the more conical "beehive" before settling on high school dropouts with white lips and Baltimore diner waitresses. To create your own bouffant, follow these simple steps:

1. The hair must be "lived in," unwashed or lightly "grungy." If you're a clean teen, some setting lotion or a coating of hairspray can provide traction.

2. Pop can–size rollers or bigger are a must. Either "sleep" in these or sit under a hairdryer if you live in a salon.

3. Section off the front of the hair from ear to ear. Divide the front hair into two sections and put the back of the hair into a high ponytail.

4. Backcomb ponytail. Also known as "ratting" or "teasing," the fine art of combing hair back toward the head creates a rat's nest of frizzy, matted hair that less resembles human hair than wet cotton candy. This gives the bulk to your bouffant.

5. Use a bristle brush to begin smoothing the top layer of hair around the mass you've created and secure the ends with a hairpin.

6. Realize at this point you have no idea what you're doing as large chunks of your matted hair start coming out in your hands. Go to a proper salon and have someone fix what you've done.

9. Repeat with the other side and secure with hairpins.

8. Grab one of the front sections. Mist liberally with hairspray. Pull upward at an angle, then sweep around the bun.

7. After the trained beautician creates a rounded shape, she secures the sides with hairpins. Hairspray at will.

10. Douse the entire head with the remainder of the hairspray can. Add bejeweled accessories if you're a classy society lady. Add a zip gun or spider eggs if you're a wrong-side-of-the-tracks delinquent.

Note: Remember to wrap the head in tissue paper and sleep in a seated position to preserve your hairstyle. A majestic bouffant is worth a little sleep deprivation!

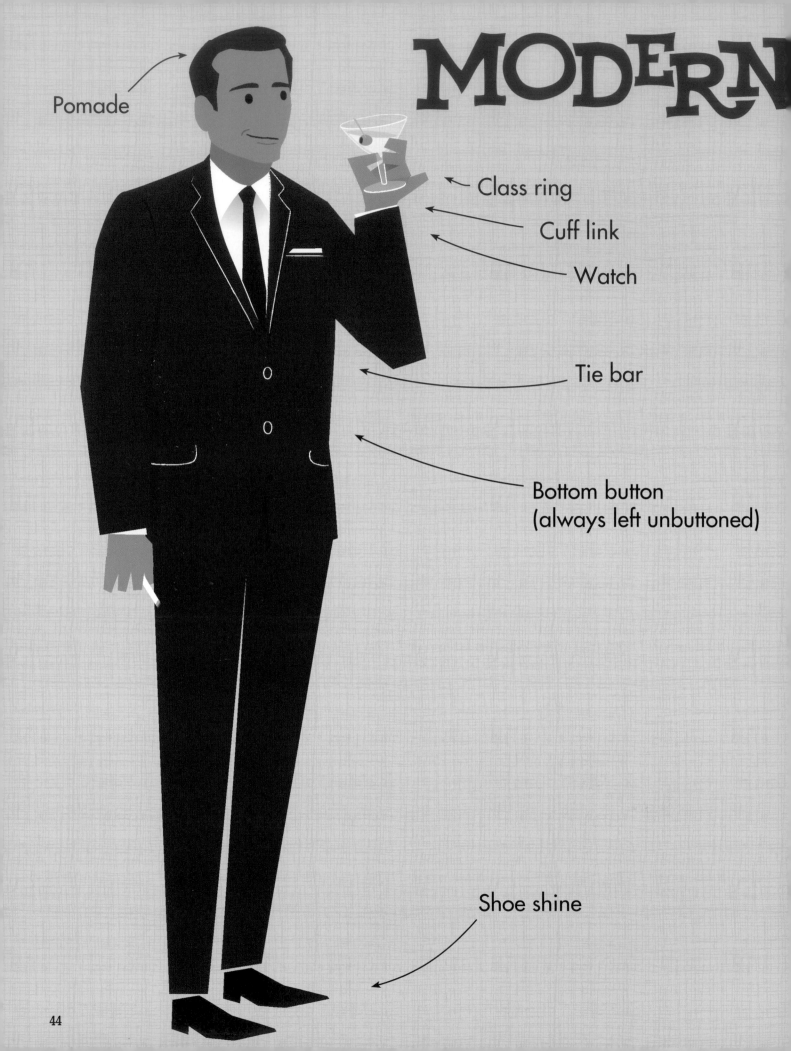

Pomade

MODERN

Class ring

Cuff link

Watch

Tie bar

Bottom button
(always left unbuttoned)

Shoe shine

ANATOMY

Glamorous Lady™ Strength-Reinforced, No-Slip, Rubber-Tipped Aluminum Hairpins: Perfect for use with Glamorous Lady™ shampoo, conditioning rinse, hairspray, comb set, flat brush, curling iron, flat iron, curlers, hairnet, color tint, relaxer, barrettes, headband, wiglette, and blow dryer

LuxoReal™ Extending and Plumping False Eyelashes in Arabian Night Black for Evening and Party Wear: *Because Batting Your Eyelashes Gets You What You Want*

Form-Lift AeroStreamline™ Bra with Patented Youth-Flex Molding Bandeaux: *The Übermensch of Brassieres Will Make Your Bosoms Fly Up, Up, and So On*

French-Made Nylon and Latex Comfort Girdle with Ultimate Support and Structure: *Accentuate Your Curves, Except the Curves of Your Stomach, Hips, and Thighs*

Midnight Secretary™ Sheer Satin- and Polyester-Blend Body Contour Underskirt Slip: *It's the Inner Petals of the Flower That Need the Most Protection* (not pictured)

Young Miss Modern™ Sensuous Garter Featuring Proven Ultra-Hold Elastic and Pressed Oriental Lace: *Thigh Sweat Shouldn't Be the Only Thing Holding Your Stockings in Place*

Luxurious Short 'n' Shapely™ Haute Couture Silk-Like No-Seam Nylon Stockings with Perfect Measured Fit and Form for All Leg Shapes and Contours: *Santa Can't Wait to Stuff These Stockings*

Exotic 100% Italian Leather Stiletto Skyscraper Pumps with Comfort Ridges and European Narrow-Toe Technology: *Make the Walk to His Office a Walk Through the Clouds*

RICH SOMMER on bow ties

The first bow tie I can recall wearing voluntarily was to my junior prom. It bore a Looney Tunes Tasmanian Devil print, which happily matched my sweet cummerbund. It was your standard rental bow tie, the kind that clips around the back of your neck. The pre-tied kind. The kind that assumes you are an idiot and have no idea how to tie a simple bow tie. I mean, come on! Who can't tie their own BOW TIE?

Just kidding. No one knows how to tie a bow tie these days. No one, except for slightly off-kilter older men and, lucky for me, costume dressers on TV shows.

Man, I was pretty cocky when we did the *Mad Men* pilot. I tied my long tie with ease. I had read a piece in *People* magazine several years earlier about the Shelby knot and had committed it to memory. Never mind that it wasn't period perfect— if you're watching the show and giving a shit about my tie knot in the pilot, please reconsider how you're channeling your energy—but it was good.

Aaron Staton couldn't even tie his long tie. He didn't know how. Boy, I ribbed him. I have some great pictures of Vincent Kartheiser tying it for him. We sure let him have it. Ha ha.

Then it came time to do the rest of the series, and I was told in my fitting that I would be wearing bow ties. Uh-oh.

In all fairness, tying a long tie is still a pretty easy-to-access part of male DNA. That bow-tie skill evolved right out of us around 1960. Let's just say that Aaron easily figured out how to tie his long tie, while I was watching YouTube videos and cramping up my hands trying to learn.

Fun Fact #1: Tying a bow tie is just like tying your shoe.

Fun Fact #2: Bullshit, unless you are upside-down and tying said shoe from inside said shoe. And the laces are super thick and have to look good.

If anyone tries to tell you that it's like tying your shoe, they are either misguided, have incredible spatial skills, or are lying and can't wait to see you sweat and struggle. In my case, I'm more inclined to believe it was the latter.

So, for the first two seasons of the show, I had someone else tie my ties for me. Which meant the shot could have been set up, lights on, film rolling, and we would still have to wait for Jagweed to get his tie tied for him. Let's just say, I wasn't impressing anyone.

After two seasons of this, including having a tie-tying rendezvous with Janie Bryant preceding any award show red carpet, I got fed up. I was done being embarrassed. I needed to learn how to do it on my own.

So, on the morning of the 2008 Emmys, I sat at my computer and watched video after video of people tying their ties. I mean, for two hours, I sat there. After several failed attempts and tons of hand stretches, I got it. And when I got it, I GOT it. It just made sense all of a sudden. I untied and retied. I did it again. Then I did it without a mirror. Perfect.

I could tie my own damn tie.

So I showed up to the Emmys, tie tied. Michael Gladis immediately asked who tied my tie for me, since he's one of those off-kilter old men who knows how to do it.

"I did," I said.

He replied, "Bullshit."

And I said, "I hate you," and walked away, which is how all of our conversations end.

I showed him at the after party how I could tie it without a mirror. He patted me on the back and

said condescendingly, "Good for you," which is another way many of our conversations end.

My point is: I learned how to tie a bow tie between seasons two and three. When I showed up for season three, I saw a bunch of clip-on bow ties.

"What the hell are these?" I asked Janie.

"Your ties," she said.

"Why are they all clip-ons?" I asked.

"Because it's 1963," she said. "Styles changed."*

"But I learned how to tie a tie!" I said. Or yelled. I don't remember.

"That's nice," she said.

Sigh.

So, I know how to tie a bow tie. The skill still comes in handy for fancy affairs, or for helping some other poor bastard who hasn't spent the requisite hours in front of a book or computer screen, destroying his fingers.

And I have good news for you: I'm gonna share the secret. I'm going to do for you what no one did for me. Here, step-by-step, is how to tie your own bow tie:

1. Hang the tie around your neck, with one side a little longer than the other.

2. Cross the ends, and pull the one side up over the other one.

3. Do a little loopy thing, and put the first side up, kinda crinkly, in front of your neck.

4. Take the other side and put it over that one and sort of stick it behind.

5. Stuff that end through the tiny hole at the back of the crinkly part, and pull it through.

6. Pull the ends. Not the folded ends, but the other ones.

7. You're done!

1. Apply a base foundation to cover all imperfections and to establish an even facial tone. You want your face to be like an idealized moon—pale, crater-free, and waiting for a man to land on it. (An American man, thank you, not a Godless Communist.)

2. Use a small dot of rouge on your cheeks for color. Be careful, as there is a big difference between a dot and a prostitute mark. For more natural color, pinch the skin, making sure to break some capillaries. The more pain you're in, the more beautiful you'll look in the mirror (after wiping away the tears).

3. Lightly dust your eyelids with face powder. Use a neutral-colored eyeshadow and sweep this from the lash line to brow bone. Then apply a brighter shade—sparkle pool chlorine blue, for example—below your crease. All this work will ensure you look as though you're not wearing eyeshadow at all.

4. With your eye pencil, brush slowly along your lash line with small movements. This is known as "feathering." Think of it as though you dipped a baby chick in black powder, and then rubbed that baby chick's backside on your lash line.

5. Apply mascara, using a zigzag pattern through your lashes from the base to the tip. Wait at least 10 seconds before applying another coat.

6. Apply lipstick evenly, making sure to create a bow on the top of your lips that will say, "I'm a present to be unwrapped—a present of mood swings, judgment, and a necessitated allowance of a few thousand dollars a month." Note: The higher the bow, the higher the sophistication and age (and necessitated allowance).

7. Last, take out your framed pictures of Jacqueline Kennedy and Mamie Eisenhower. Compare your face to theirs. If the resemblance is more to the latter than the former, start over.

MAKEUP TIPS
for Young Moderns

See? It's actually easier than you thought, isn't it? I know my directions are a little tough to follow without pictures, but keep trying. You'll get it eventually. And if all else fails, just pretend you're tying your shoe. That works every time.

—Rich Sommer

* I asked Aaron, Michael, and Janie if they were okay with their mentions in this story. Aaron reminded me that he knew how to tie a tie, just not the knot the costumers wanted. Michael wanted me to tell you that he's as big a jerk as I make him out to be (yes, he is). And Janie said that styles didn't actually change. She gave me the clip-ons because she was sick of tying my tie for me.

ARTS & LEISURE

Broadway: 1960

Despite competition from TV and movies, 1960s Broadway was still in a relative golden age: Rodgers and Hammerstein were cranking out the last of their hits, Neil Simon was one year away from his first Broadway play, and somewhere in England twelve-year-old Andrew Lloyd Webber was putting his pet cats in leotards. Here's what you could have seen on any given night on Broadway in 1960:

Bye Bye Birdie—A knowing but sanitized parody of the teen-idol epidemic, *Bye Bye Birdie* proved that once upon a time Broadway actually had its finger on the pulse of youth culture (sort of). The name of the show's title character, Conrad Birdie, was obviously a play on Conway Twitty, but the role spoofed all teen dreams, including Elvis and Fabian. In his big break, Dick Van Dyke starred as Conrad's manager, and *West Side Story*'s Chita Rivera played his Latin love interest, "Spanish" Rose. When the movie version came out three years later, Van Dyke reprised his role, and Rose was played by the well-known Hispanic actress . . . Janet Leigh. Susan Watson played the teenage ingénue on Broadway and went on to a decent career, but was pretty much lost to the dustbin of history—she just wasn't Ann-Margret.

Fiorello!—The 1960 Pulitzer Prize in Drama was won not by blockbuster favorite *The Sound of Music* nor by Stephen Sondheim's classic *Gypsy*, but by a musical that starred the dad from *Happy Days* as the guy who lent his name to New York's third largest airport. Tom Bosley won a Tony Award playing Great Depression–era mayor Fiorello LaGuardia, but despite critical accolades and its pioneering use of a titular exclamation point (presaging both *Oh! Calcutta!* and *Mamma Mia!*), *Fiorello!* has not once been revived on Broadway since it closed in 1961.

The Sound of Music—Everyone could agree: Rodgers and Hammerstein wrote great tunes, Nazis were bad, and icy Aryan baronesses should not stand in the way of nuns and hunky sea captains. Plus, once the public saw Mary Martin play Sister Maria, it could collectively forget that she had just spent a few years pretending to be a tights-wearing, flying, prepubescent boy in *Peter Pan*.

My Fair Lady—Wildly popular by 1960, the Lerner and Loewe musical had been running for four years and would go on for two more. Between this and the still-to-come 1964 movie *Mary Poppins*, Americans became convinced England was overrun with Cockney chimney sweeps and soot-covered flower girls who said things like "Gahrn, guv'nah! Oy've got a tuppence wit' me farthing, oy do!"

Camelot—Lerner and Loewe's follow-up musical, *Camelot*, opened on December 3, 1960—just in time to become the Official Metaphor for the Kennedy White House. Richard Burton, Julie Andrews, and Robert Goulet starred in the musical that reflected a simpler time in America's history: before the assassination of JFK, before the escalation of the Vietnam War, and before the beginnings of Goulet's mustache.

THE CHARLESTON

The Charleston was a runaway hit dance that defined a decade. It first came to national attention in 1923 with a tune called "The Charleston" in the Broadway show *Runnin' Wild* by composer/pianist James P. Johnson. But any song with a fairly quick beat and a 4/4 time signature can underscore your impromptu performance.

1. Step back on the right leg.

2. Swing the left leg back in a kicking motion. (Keep that ankle loose!)

3. Bring the left foot forward and step, returning to the starting position.

4. Kick the right foot forward, keeping it loose.

5. Repeat.

The arms are key…This motion is where the term "flapper" comes from.

1. The right leg goes back first, the left arm will go up first, and vice versa. Always keep the arms complementary to the feet.

2. Crook your elbows 90 degrees.

3. Hold your arms high and as they swing let them move in circular motions to the right and left. Keep it big and exaggerated.

Once you and your partner have the knack for the basic step, throw in a couple dazzlers—moves like Savoy Kicks and Freezes. You'll have plenty of time to look those up on your own with the time you save not having children.

THE TWIST was the first truly international dance craze at the dawn of the 1960s. Launched by the eponymous B-side of Hank Ballard's 1959 single "Teardrops on Your Letter," kingmaker Dick Clark thought raunchy Ballard was a tough sell to his teenage audience and tapped squeaky-clean Chubby Checker to cover the song a year later. Released in the summer of 1960, Checker's version of "The Twist" became number one on the singles chart in the USA in 1960 and then again in 1962.

Further Twist Discography

"The Twist" by Hank Ballard and the Midnighters (No. 28, 1960)

"The Twist" by Chubby Checker (No. 1, 1960; No. 1, 1962)

"Let's Twist Again" by Chubby Checker (No. 8, 1961)

"Twistin' USA" by Danny and the Juniors (No. 20, 1961)

"Slow Twistin'" by Chubby Checker (No. 3, 1962)

"Peppermint Twist—Part 1" by Joey Dee and the Starliters (No. 1, 1962)

"Hey, Let's Twist" by Joey Dee and the Starliters (No. 20, 1962)

"Dear Lady Twist" by Gary "U.S." Bonds (No. 9, 1962)

"Twist, Twist, Señora" by Gary "U.S." Bonds (No. 9, 1962)

"Twistin' Postman" by the Marvelettes (No. 34, 1962)

"Twistin' the Night Away" by Sam Cooke (No. 9, 1962)

"Twist and Shout" by the Isley Brothers (No. 17, 1962)

"Twist-Her" by Bill Black's Combo (No. 26, 1962)

"Soul Twist" by King Curtis and the Noble Knights (No. 17, 1962)

"Bristol Twistin' Annie" by the Dovells (No. 27, 1962)

"Percolator (Twist)" by Billie Joe and the Checkmates (No. 10, 1962)

"Twist It Up" by Chubby Checker (No. 25, 1963)

"Twist and Shout" by the Beatles (No. 2, 1964)

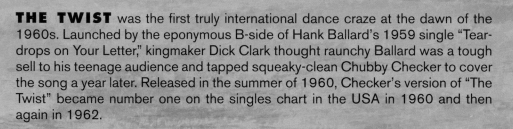

These are just the ones that charted in the United States; the clearance rack of history has dozens more cracked platters…"The Chicken Twist," "The Headhunter Twist," "Bei Mir Twist Du Schoen" (aka "The Challah Twist"), etc.

JAI ALAI

Baseball always claims to be America's pastime, but in shadier corners of America's consciousness, it's hard to beat the emotional thrill of money for nothing: gambling.

Sure, Americans are free to rush to the racetracks to place wagers on horse and dog racing, but if you want beast-free sport with on-site betting your only option is the fastest game in the world…jai alai!

Born in the sixteenth century among the Basques of Spain, jai alai (meaning "merry festival") was introduced to America at the 1904 St. Louis World's Fair. During the 1920s, jai alai courts, known as "frontons," sprang up in Miami, Chicago, and New Orleans, but the sport only flourished in Florida, where gambling on the game was not prohibited.

The rules of jai alai are similar to handball, except played with a ball (called a "pelota") that is harder and heavier than a golf ball and tossed against the wall by wicker baskets (known as "cestas") that are strapped to a player's right arm. Bettors place wagers on matches that take place between groups of singles competitors or doubles teams, who can earn the gamblers a payout by either winning, placing (as runner-up), or showing (as second runner-up).

Jai alai holds the Guinness world record for fastest game in the world, with the speediest pelotas clocking in at over 150 miles per hour.

Midcentury Novel Cheat Sheet

Fake your way though any cocktail party conversation without wasting valuable drinking time reading. Commit these to memory and you'll be into that Columbia coed's pants and/or that corner office (depending on what kind of scene you're operating) with your winning "well-read" ways:

Rabbit, Run by John Updike (1960)—Sex leads to marriage leads to sex outside marriage leads to death leads back to marriage.

Atlas Shrugged by Ayn Rand (1957)—A strident defense of capitalism and individualism told in the form of a hack sci-fi novel.

Meditations in an Emergency by Frank O'Hara (1957)—Contemplation on love, sex, and meaning in mid-twentieth-century New York City, without much hope for any of the above.

The Sound and the Fury by William Faulkner (1929)—A Southern family falls into ruin in a virtuosic narrative that shuttles between the perspectives of a Harvard student and some "simple" kid.

The Feminine Mystique by Betty Friedan (1963)—What happens when you send gals to college and then make them quit their jobs for hubby and kids?

Sex and the Single Girl by Helen Gurley Brown (1962)—How to be an unrepentant—yet Machiavellian—slut from the woman who later founded *Cosmo*.

Silent Spring by Rachel Carson (1962)—Remember DDT? No? Then thank Ms. Carson. (Some people also want to thank her for the global resurgence of malaria, but that's another story . . .)

Throw around references to **The Hidden Persuaders** (1957), **The Organization Man** (1956), and **White Collar** (1951) . . . the content doesn't so much matter as much as the fact that you are aware of these books' existence and therefore hip to the sham of modern society.

HORSEMANSHIP FOR THE HAPPILY MARRIED HOUSEWIFE

Sometimes your gallop just isn't what it used to be. And neither is your horsemanship. But bettering your trots, cantors, and jumps is as easy as putting a roast in the oven at 5:00 p.m. for your husband, who you expect home from work at 6:00, but who doesn't actually arrive home until 10:00, with absolutely no explanation of why. Easy as that!

Always come to the barn prepared with a plan, never a timetable. And stick to the plan. Don't change because a "meeting" comes up or a "mysterious late-night conference call" has to happen or a sudden "flashback to the past" occurs.

To make a horse's trot longer and bigger, drive forward into a more constant connection. The horse and you are the ones that should have the connection. Not the horse and his secretary.

When taking jumps for the first time with your horse, trot over the poles and take things slow, because sometimes things are difficult for your horse to understand, like remembering how to approach a cavalletti or how not to sleep with your child's teacher. Trotting over jumps will also improve your horse's balance and coordination.

Never let your horse turn away and reapproach the fence. If you allow this, you're teaching your horse how to say no, and that's not all right. He made a commitment to jump with you in sickness and in health, till death do you part, and he *has* to honor that commitment. Start with small jumps so that he can go over them from a standstill.

When finishing for the day, make sure to reward your horse for his good work by grooming him and washing his feet. This helps to cement the bond between horse and rider. But then find that stable boy from earlier and tenderly kiss him in front of your horse, just to make sure he knows who's in charge.

If a horse had too much bend in his neck during the shoulder-in, try this correction: As you come around the corner, let him think he is going onto the diagonal but ask him to do a shoulder-in down the long side instead. Sometimes it's good to play mind games since you know what's best, and he's just going to give you attitude if you're straightforward.

See how your horse is reacting. Feel how he is feeling. Even if he couldn't care less how you are feeling. You demotivate a horse to work hard when he is tired. Just like when you get demotivated when you smell perfume that isn't yours on one of your husband's shirts.

If your horse fidgets with his head, don't react or pull. Stay quiet. For the moment, keep your hands low and ask for more bend to stretch the soreness out of his muscles. Later on, use his money to redecorate your living room to make up for his insubordination.

In midcentury America, nothing is more romantic, more sophisticated, more *ooh-la-la* than France. Poodles. Dressing. Singing nuns.* Authenticity is secondary to the mythical je ne sais quoi of Frenchness.

No need to trudge through years of language lessons, the following song has French phrases and words you already use in English. Accompany yourself using any melody you can think of that sounds "French" enough to you.

Chanson d'Amour Decoupage

L'amour est un cul-de-sac
Avec deux maison et Honoré de Balzac
Monte-blanc coeur est a la carte
Mon aide-de-camp est avant garde

Chorus:
Au revoir, mon bon vivant!
Nouveau riche chauffeur
Déjà vu au soirée
Avec mon au pair

Verse:
Je t'aime mais macramé mêlée
Vous aimez le foie gras sommelier
Nous sommes bric-à-brac vinaigrette
Enfant terrible eau de toilette

Beaucoup après moi, le deluge
Mon pièce de résistance au jus
Droit du seigneur, cherchez la femme
Votre Grand Prix est t'aime

Respondez s'il vous plaît
Respondez s'il vous plaît!

Love is a long road
With mansions and honorable men's parts
My pure heart is as it seems
The assistance it receives is from the theater

Chorus:
Farewell, lothario!
Freshly paid machinery operator
I saw you at the party
With a young lady

Verse:
I love to argue in your style
You love the liver organizer
We do not get along
Whose perfume is that?

I left a big puddle
Of very nice gravy
You have the right to look for me
You have won my love

Contact me at your earliest convenience
I am waiting!

ooh la la!

*Actually Belgian.

56

MARK ROTHKO AND THE BURDEN OF FAME

Although best known for his "smudgy squares," that particular style came late in Mark Rothko's career—first appearing in 1946. In those blocks of raw pigment color mixed with binder, methodically burnished layer after layer onto oversized canvases, Rothko found what he called "the breath of life" and infinite possibilities not limited by representational forms. He urged viewers of his 1950 and 1951 solo shows to stand very close to the huge paintings and be enveloped in the fields of color. The 1952 "Fifteen Americans" show at the MoMA formally heralded the abstract artists, showing Rothko alongside Jackson Pollock and William Baziotes.

Rothko's star began to rise, but he had an uneasy relationship with his increasing success. Despite the welcome relief after decades of financial struggle, he railed against the moneyed trend chasers who bought his work to stick over their mantels and impress their neighbors. When *Fortune* magazine named a Rothko painting as a good investment, his longtime friend Barnett Newman called him a sellout motivated by bourgeois aspirations.

After an inspirational tour of the Michelangelo room in the library at San Lorenzo, Rothko became increasingly preoccupied with controlling how his work was displayed. He yearned to create intimate, chapel-like spaces free of distraction and natural light where the viewer could be absorbed into the fields of color and meaning. When in 1958 architect Philip Johnson offered Rothko the commission of murals for the Four Seasons restaurant in the modern Seagram Building (designed by Johnson and Mies van der Rohe), it seemed like a perfect opportunity. Even as it appealed to Rothko's vanity and ego, he still planned to paint "something that will ruin the appetite of every son of a bitch who ever eats in that room."

Over the course of three months, Rothko completed forty paintings for the Seagram Building—three full series in dark red and brown. However, something changed after Rothko ate in the ultra-luxe dining room for the first time. He returned his advance and declined the commission. The paintings intended for the Four Seasons were put in storage for years before being sold off to separate collectors. His reasons were never made clear.

Rothko didn't care for the younger generation of Pop artists, who the rich collectors increasingly preferred at the dawn of the 1960s. Lichtenstein, Rosenquist, and (former advertising illustrator) Andy Warhol. He labeled the Pop movement artists "charlatans and young opportunists" and found their work valueless and glib.

On February 25, 1970, Rothko's assistant found him lying dead on the kitchen floor, having slashed his arms with razors and overdosed on antidepressants.

PHRASES FOR WELL-MEANING SQUARES

Just because you're a corporate suit working for The Man (for a pretty impressive salary, to boot) doesn't mean you aren't "hep" to the struggles for civil rights. Try these choice phrases to connect to the zeitgeist—and to your new comrades-in-arms:

◄ "I have all of Harry Belafonte's albums."

◄ "Let's say I wanted to sell you a television. What would be the best way to do that…for equality, I mean?"

◄ "Man, our income disparity is so jive."

◄ "I never believed in the Dred Scott decision."

◄ "My housekeeper and I really get along."

◄ "That 'I Have a Dream' speech was so moving. It reminds me, I keep having this recurring dream of my mother chasing me with a huge pair of scissors…What do you think it means?"

◄ "Say, didn't I see your kid getting bused into my kid's school?"

◄ "How many ascots should I pack for the Freedom Ride?"

◄ "I was known as the Medgar Evers of my Princeton eating club."

◄ "Say hey, Willie Mays! And by that, I want to make it clear that I do not think you are actually Willie Mays."

◄ "Do you happen to have a memoir of your poor but proud upbringing? I have an editor friend at the *Atlantic Monthly* and they go crazy for that garbage."

◄ "For the next spiritual, you mind if I take a turn on the ol' tambourine? It's okay, I brought one from home."

DOs AND DON'Ts

DO memorize Allen Ginsburg's "Howl."

DON'T recite it to the tune of "Hello Muddah, Hello Faddah."

DO discuss the escalating situation in Vietnam.

DON'T offer to do an impression of your Chinese dry cleaner.

DO mention that you think Bob Dylan is the most exciting new artist you've seen in years.

DON'T add, "But I think he's Jewish."

DO read Ralph Ellison's *Invisible Man.*

DON'T see the movie *The Invisible Man* to just "get the gist of it."

psychoanalysis goes pop!

In 1956, Sigmund Freud would have celebrated his hundredth birthday and the occasion sparked a boom of public interest in psychiatry.

Of course there were plenty of academic responses, and even these were hugely popular. Americans ran to the bookstores when Herbert Marcuse's critique of Freud, *Eros and Civilization*, was first published in paperback in 1961. And it's no wonder why; Marcuse laid the philosophical groundwork for the Free Love movement just a few years later by tying sexual liberation to political liberation.

America's novelists had wrestled with psychiatry and mental illness for decades, but no book brought psychiatry to bear on culture as harshly as Ken Kesey's *One Flew Over the Cuckoo's Nest*. The novel was a bestseller in 1962 and it spawned a popular Broadway adaptation in 1963. The book's devastating critique of conformism and the institutionalization of society made it a central part of the '60s countercultural canon.

The American obsession with psychiatry definitely wasn't limited to high art and intellectualism. By the mid-'50s both *Mademoiselle* and *Good Housekeeping* featured articles and columns about psychoanalysis. In 1955, Entertaining Comics, the publisher of *Tales from the Crypt* and *The Vault of Horror*, published a one-off issue simply titled *Psychoanalysis #1*. Folksinger Katie Lee released two full albums comprised entirely of psychotherapy-related musical comedy: 1957's *Songs of Couch and Consultation* and 1960's *Life Is Just a Bed of Neuroses* featured songs such as "Repressed Hostility Blues," "The Ballad for Group Therapy," and "We Must Adjust."

For all of psychiatry's influence on popular culture, America's neuroses shone most brightly on the silver screen. The most direct nod to the couch's steady infiltration of the American home was John Huston's melodramatic biopic titled *Freud: The Secret Passion*. An ailing Montgomery Clift starred in the title role. A much more qualified portrayal of the psychiatrist in society came in 1963 with *Captain Newman, MD*. Gregory Peck's Dr. Newman was a wartime psychiatrist, treating World War II veterans for post-traumatic stress, long before the phrase entered popular vocabulary. This was an image of the psychiatrist as benevolent caregiver, in a constant battle with the ills of the world.

These films might have been in some part a reaction to 1960's *Psycho*, which gave voice to the persistent worry that no matter how much we try to deal with our mother issues, there'll always be a knife-wielding dead-mama's boy inside all of us.

MODERNIZING THE CHURCH

In 1962, just about every Roman Catholic American went to church on Sunday, ate fish on Friday, and aside from hanging a picture of Kennedy in the living room, mostly kept their faith an arm's length from their politics. Priests recited the Mass only in Latin and with their backs turned to the parishioners. But by 1965, the reforms of the Second Vatican Council changed almost everything.

During those three short years, the bishops in Rome made a series of sweeping changes. The most obvious changes had the priests turning away from the altar toward the pews and speaking in a language that churchgoers could understand. The council decided that the laity ought to have a bigger role in the Church, and these changes were a sort of liturgical welcome mat, inviting them in.

Slightly less obvious, though quite a bit more significant, was the council's call for the Church and for individual Catholics to embrace the modern world, rather than trying to be above it. As the council wrote, "The joys and the hopes, the griefs and the anxieties of the men of this age, especially those who are poor or in any way afflicted, these are the joys and hopes, the griefs and anxieties of the followers of Christ." This call to action brought the Church further into the spirit of social action that was sweeping the country. After Vatican II, it wasn't uncommon to see your parish priest marching in an antiwar demonstration while strumming an acoustic guitar instead of hunched over an altar and wheezing a barely audible Mass.

New Yorkers were particularly sensitive to these changes, thanks to their famously traditional archbishop. Francis Cardinal Spellman, Archbishop of New York, had attended the council and was sharply critical of many of its reforms. He opposed vernacular reading of the liturgy, famously declaring that "no change will get past the Statue of Liberty," while also criticizing the social activist activities of priests such as David Kirk, Philip and Daniel Berrigan, and other clergy who sought to bring Catholic teachings to bear on the Civil Rights Movement.

DREAM CAR FOR THE RISING EXECUTIVE

This is America. What you drive shows the rest of the world that you matter, that you're more important than they will ever be, and also that you will never, ever die. What features should you look for in your next automobile in order to cause gnawing envy in all onlookers and reaffirm your own sense of ever-ballooning importance?

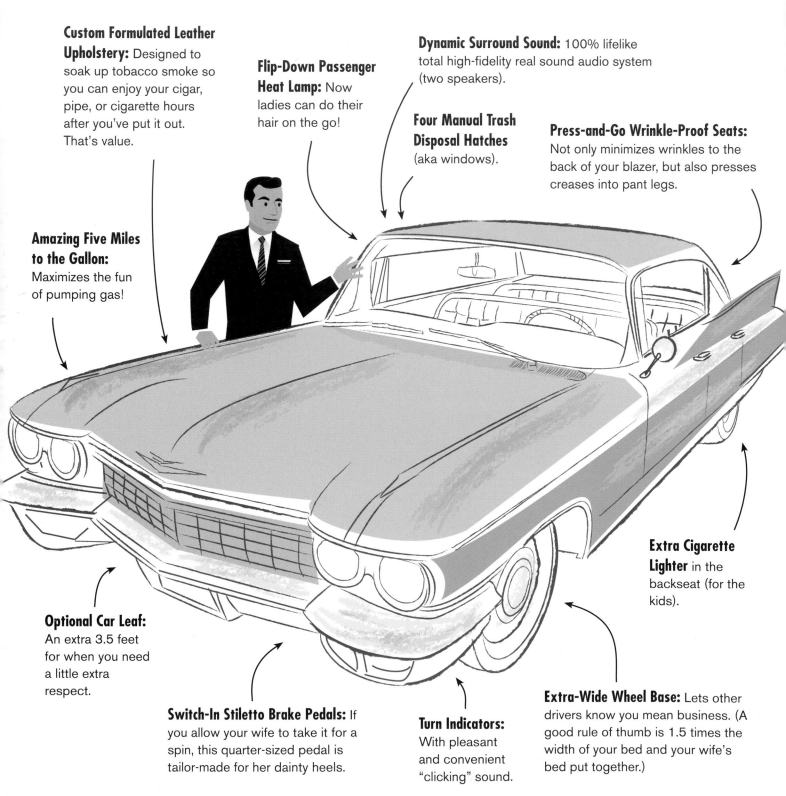

Custom Formulated Leather Upholstery: Designed to soak up tobacco smoke so you can enjoy your cigar, pipe, or cigarette hours after you've put it out. That's value.

Flip-Down Passenger Heat Lamp: Now ladies can do their hair on the go!

Dynamic Surround Sound: 100% lifelike total high-fidelity real sound audio system (two speakers).

Four Manual Trash Disposal Hatches (aka windows).

Press-and-Go Wrinkle-Proof Seats: Not only minimizes wrinkles to the back of your blazer, but also presses creases into pant legs.

Amazing Five Miles to the Gallon: Maximizes the fun of pumping gas!

Optional Car Leaf: An extra 3.5 feet for when you need a little extra respect.

Switch-In Stiletto Brake Pedals: If you allow your wife to take it for a spin, this quarter-sized pedal is tailor-made for her dainty heels.

Turn Indicators: With pleasant and convenient "clicking" sound.

Extra Cigarette Lighter in the backseat (for the kids).

Extra-Wide Wheel Base: Lets other drivers know you mean business. (A good rule of thumb is 1.5 times the width of your bed and your wife's bed put together.)

The International Style

While it wasn't the first city to sprout skyscrapers, New York City owes much of its iconic image to its forest of tall buildings. Gotham's skyscrapers, constructed in the nineteenth and early twentieth centuries, were chiefly brick-and-mortar odes to the captains of industry who financed their construction. Their design demanded exquisite decoration and shape, and the results exuded grandeur. But the real archetypal New York skyscraper of today—that featureless, rectangular, enormous glass monolith—took off in the rush of postwar corporate optimism, through an architectural movement known as the "international style."

First used by German modernists in the 1920s and then promulgated by the Museum of Modern Art for a 1932 exhibition, the term *international style* connoted huge, functional edifices without any flourishes or ornamentation. Sleek. Stark. Minimal. Nothing appeared that didn't have a recognizable purpose—no more, no less. Or, as the quintessential international style architect Ludwig Mies van der Rohe (1886–1969) famously dictated, "Less is more."

In addition to Mies (note: throw around the adjective "Miesian" at your next cocktail party architecture discussion, and everyone will think you're a real authority), big wheels in the movement included the architects Philip Johnson (1906–2005), Walter Gropius (1883–1969), and Le Corbusier (real name: Charles-Édouard Jeanneret-Gris, 1887–1965).

Testaments to the style's dominance stab through the New York skyline: Mies's Seagram Building; the Lever House by Gordon Bunshaft; the MetLife Building (formerly the Pan Am Building) by Emery Roth & Sons (with Gropius as consultant); and the United Nations Headquarters, designed by Oscar Niemeyer (in partial collaboration with Le Corbusier).

By 1960, the international style was at its heyday—and creeping toward its obsolescence. Eventually, the popularity of severe form-following-function gave way to the smirking, reference-filled dazzle of postmodernism. The architect and critic Robert Venturi, writing in 1966, may have had the last word on Mies and his fellow international stylists: "Less is a bore."

WRITE YOUR OWN FOLK SONG

The reason most folk music is so atrocious is that it was written by the people.* Luckily, in our era of push-button ease and ultra-convenience, science has come up with a foolproof method for the next time you find yourself at the open mic down at the coffeehouse with a heart full of modern malaise and a mind blank of metaphors.

First, master these chords:

G major	D major	C major	A minor
OOO	XOO	X O O	XO O

2 1 3   1 3 2   3 2 1   2 3 1

Now, follow the lyric chart:

FOLK SONG THEME

Protest! (things you don't like)

Your Loneliness (why you are sad)

Nature (mountains, railroads)

Politics	War	Work	A Woman	Several Women	Flowers	Animals
oppression	bomb	crops	Mary	harem	impatiens	lion
rights	desecration	shops	fairy	scare them	hyacinth	giraffe
the people	pain	daytime	scary	ignored	rose	bear
zoning laws	wonderment	sublime	hairy	untoward	Amazonian corpse blossom	ants

*Joke stolen, appreciatively, from Tom Lehrer.

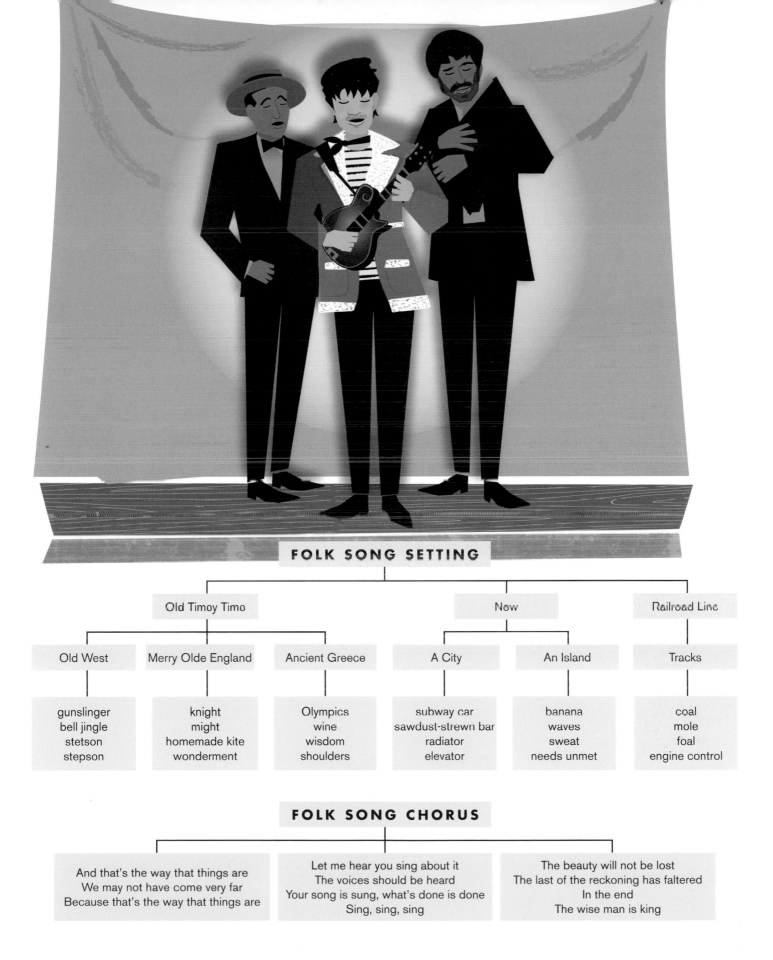

FOLK SONG SETTING

Old Timoy Timo

- Old West
  - gunslinger
  - bell jingle
  - stetson
  - stepson
- Merry Olde England
  - knight
  - might
  - homemade kite
  - wonderment
- Ancient Greece
  - Olympics
  - wine
  - wisdom
  - shoulders

Now

- A City
  - subway car
  - sawdust-strewn bar
  - radiator
  - elevator
- An Island
  - banana
  - waves
  - sweat
  - needs unmet

Railroad Line

- Tracks
  - coal
  - mole
  - foal
  - engine control

FOLK SONG CHORUS

And that's the way that things are
We may not have come very far
Because that's the way that things are

Let me hear you sing about it
The voices should be heard
Your song is sung, what's done is done
Sing, sing, sing

The beauty will not be lost
The last of the reckoning has faltered
In the end
The wise man is king

Congratulations, you've now taken society's oppressors down a peg in a room full of people who already agree with you. If male, awkwardly shamble off stage. If female, remove clothes.

TRAVEL

Seduction at 20,000 feet

Look for these subtle hints from your stewardess to sense her level of "gameness":

✦ Casually slips off your wedding ring as she hands you a tiny pack of peanuts.

✦ Doesn't report you to the captain if you loosen your tie a little bit.

✦ Uniform pillbox hat worn extra-jauntily askew.

✦ Gives you the premium 12-year-old single-malt complimentary scotch, not that shoddy 8-year-old single-malt complimentary scotch.

✦ Gives you Li'l Pilot wings with her phone number carved into the plastic.

✦ Points out the really hip landmarks as you fly over them, not the square ones everyone else gets to see.

Lutèce

249 East 50th Street

When the chips are down, and you feel like your assets are slipping away, this gorgeous French restaurant is a great place to get a grip. And if you need to mend fences, the expensive dinners will make even halfhearted apologies seem dear.

MARK YOUR MAN

FIRE ROSE RED

Belle Jolie

Roosevelt Hotel

Madison Avenue and 45th Street

Discretion is the watchword in this stately hotel. The dark wood holds a lot of secrets, even ones you're not ready to let out. But there's plenty of comfort here, too. Taking your shoes off in the lobby will feel like a huge relief, no matter how light your loafers.

BONWIT TELLER

Bonwit Teller

5th Avenue and 38th Street

A women's clothing boutique specializing in high-end merchandise for women who prefer to keep things at the low end. Great for a long visit or just a short detour from your regular routine.

P.J. Clarke's
3rd Avenue and 55th Street

Who needs Broadway when this laid-back Irish saloon will let you kick up your own heels? No need to keep your arms folded when you're here. Just turn on the music and fling, fling, fling!

Oyster Bar
Grand Central Station

Want to bet this belowground treasure has the best shellfish you could scrape up? We wager the seafood here will one-up anything you could dream of, and if we're wrong we'll eat our words, even if we're so stuffed we just throw them right back up again.

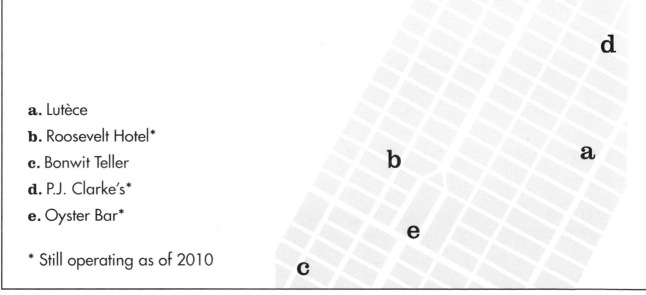

a. Lutèce

b. Roosevelt Hotel*

c. Bonwit Teller

d. P.J. Clarke's*

e. Oyster Bar*

* Still operating as of 2010

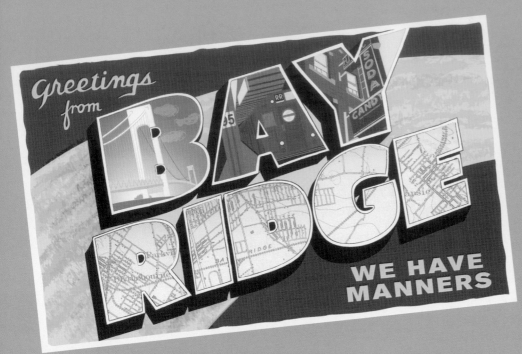

Greetings from *BAY RIDGE*

SODA CANDY

WE HAVE MANNERS

In the southwest of corner of Brooklyn, as far as you can get from Manhattan on the old RR subway line, lies the solid middle-class neighborhood of Bay Ridge. With its conservative values and strong family presence, it is not uncommon to see fourth-generation families who haven't been to "the city" in a decade.

South Bay Ridge is traditionally "Italian Bay Ridge" while the North is known as "Irish Bay Ridge," despite its being just as much Norwegian. In its heyday, approximately 200,000 first-generation Norwegians lived in the area, speaking Norwegian in the streets, stores, and at church services.

The Norwegian Constitution Day Parade, also known as the Syttende Mai (May 17) Parade, is the largest in the United States and has been celebrated annually since 1952. The parade features hundreds of people in folk dress who parade down Fifth Avenue to Leif Ericson Park where Miss Norway is crowned under a statue of Leif Ericson, which was donated by Crown Prince Olav of Norway in 1939.

Even a tight-knit, tradition-minded community can be a victim of the unrelenting hammer of progress. The controversial public works maestro Robert Moses had one of his last great victories when he displaced 7,000 Bay Ridge residents to build the Verrazano-Narrows Bridge connecting Brooklyn to Staten Island.

The Verrazano, constructed from 1959 to 1964, is still the longest suspension bridge in the United States and the sixth longest in the world. Despite vehement protests from residents and community activists, Moses demolished hundreds of homes to make way for the long bridge ramp through the heart of the neighborhood in a strip along 7th Avenue.

THE BATTLE FOR PENN STATION

The old Pennsylvania Station, built in 1910, was an architectural jewel of early twentieth-century New York City. By 1961, though, city planners were eyeing the neoclassical structure with less awe, and with more interest in the four city blocks it covered. A plan was set to raze the whole structure, move all of the station's operations underground, and free up more city blocks for new civic structures—namely, Madison Square Garden.

Such development, the project's boosters believed, would make more efficient use of valuable land and draw much-needed business to the city's center—and bail out the nearly bankrupt Pennsylvania Railroad company. Not all New Yorkers looked warmly on such civic planning though: A coalition of architects formed a protest group called AGBANY (Action Group for Better Architecture in New York), and their call to save Penn Station drew other supporters. Soon their message could be seen in newspaper ads and on picket signs at AGBANY's protest rallies: "DON'T AMPUTATE—RENOVATE!" "SAVE OUR HERITAGE!" "BE A PENN PAL!"

But AGBANY and its supporters couldn't stop the march of progress: On October 28, 1963, the demolition project began. Modernism's promise of progress, of ever improving what's come before, faced up against civic pride, and conquered it with a wrecking ball. The protestors' efforts were not all in vain, however: The entire brouhaha prompted Mayor Robert F. Wagner to establish the New York City Landmarks Preservation Commission, a body whose most celebrated accomplishment was saving Grand Central Terminal from a similar fate.

Notables in favor of knocking it down:

A. J. Greenough, president of the Pennsylvania Railroad

Irving M. Felt, president of the Madison Square Garden Corporation

Robert F. Wagner, mayor of New York (sort of; he didn't stop it)

Notables in favor of preserving it:

Ada Louise Huxtable, architecture critic for the *New York Times*

Jane Jacobs, author of *The Life and Death of Great American Cities*

The American Institute of Architects

Daniel Patrick Moynihan, Democratic senator of New York

Philip Johnson, architect

Beverly Hills Hotel

Hey, Mr. Gray Flannel Suit! Has the East Coast rat race left you searching for your old self? Try a recharge at this sun-soaked five-star getaway: the teeny-weeny-bikini scenery would make the most jaded nine-to-fiver smile. And if you're bargaining for adventure, the jet-set clientele who frequent the poolside bar will help you seal that deal.

Bonus tip: Fly TWA–their luggage service will make your dreams come true!

Hideaway at the Beach

If you've lost your tune, a jaunt to San Pedro will teach you to play piano like a maestro. An afternoon dip in the Pacific can make you feel like a new man. Short on duds? Nearby thrift stores offer plenty of cheap clothes (also make great gifts for surprise guests). Make sure to bring back some California oranges and show everyone that your trip west let you find a new squeeze.

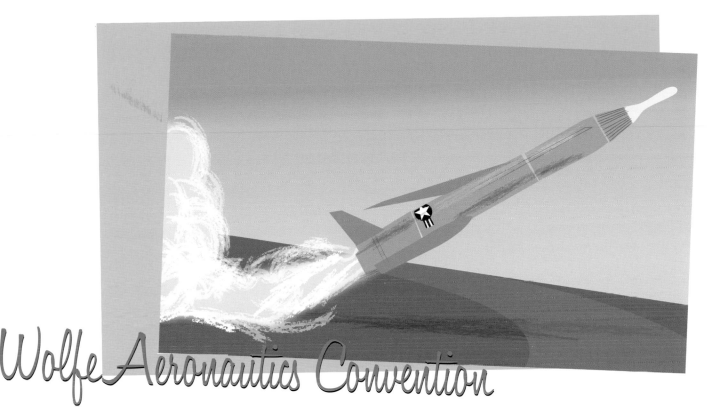

Wolfe Aeronautics Convention

Want to hitch your space-wagon to the next Alan Shepherd? Earth will stay still while you get lost in the space of some of the most brilliant minds of the atomic age. You'll want to burn all your books to make room for the new ideas you'll harvest here. And for you business typos mining for opportunities of the space-age variety, this convention will give you at least three lucky strikes.

Find Joy in the Desert

Too choked up on stress from the city to find your groove? Cruise out to a desert house in Palm Springs and cough, man. The international style architecture of these homes is so relaxing you'll be ready to hit the floor at any time. Catch up on reading, take a dip in a pool, or even just crash on the couch. The desert homes are great for lovers, foreigners, the whole family, or everyone at once.

Ugly Americans & The Eternal City

> Across the street from Terminal Station in Rome…stand five great continental hotels…to which all the travel books and vacation pamphlets direct the American tourist. They attract no one else. Walk into one of these spots on a summer night, and you might just as well have never left home. English fills the air. Bridge games go on in the lobby. For $20 a day in the Eternal City, you have bought the equivalent of a Legion convention in Detroit.
>
> —Arthur Frommer, *Europe on 5 Dollars a Day* (1957)

When World War II ended in 1945, most Europeans viewed Americans as liberators, GI Joes who strolled through the rubble of destroyed villages and offered chocolate bars to orphans. It took only two decades for boorish American tourists to overrun the slowly rebuilding Continent and destroy that goodwill forever. By 1960, GI Joe had become the Ugly American, and he wanted to know IF ANYBODY AROUND HERE SPOKE ENGLISH. ENG-UH-LISH!

Italy, meanwhile, began to exert tremendous cultural influence; it was, in the eyes of America, the land of Gina Lollobrigida, Marcello Mastroianni, and (va va va voom!) Sophia Loren. Hipsters went gaga for Italian auteurs and clogged art-house cinemas to see *La Notte* (1961) and *8½* (1963). Italian race cars like Ferrari and Maserati were just starting to make middle-aged men salivate. And the number one attraction at the 1964 World's Fair in New York was Michelangelo's *Pietà*. (It was, classily, placed on a stage covered in blue velvet and flickering lights, and visitors were shuttled past it on a moving platform.)

Naturally, Rome became a destination of choice for the American tourist eager to spend his postwar boom dollars. The must-see locations and activities:

- **VATICAN CITY:** It was, for the first and arguably last time, an exciting time to be Catholic in America. The first Catholic president had been elected in 1959, and the reforms of Vatican II were just a few short years away. But you didn't have to be Catholic to want to visit the Holy City. The art (including the *Pietà*, sans blue velvet and moving platform), the gardens, the clownfish-like Swiss Guard…All of it was designed to impress. You could spend hours just standing in St. Peter's Square looking for suspicious puffs of chimney smoke.

- **THE COLOSSEUM:** Who could spend more than a few minutes here and not want to become a gladiator? Or a chariot driver? Or the guy selling gelato at an extreme markup? Or a mob of feral cats?

- **TREVI FOUNTAIN:** Made famous by the romantic film *Three Coins in the Fountain* (1954) and its maddeningly catchy title song—legend had it that if you threw a coin into the fountain, you were destined to return to Rome. To remain in Rome longer than expected, you threw in your passport.

- **RESTAURANTS:** Italian cuisine, while mouthwateringly delicious, took some getting used to for Americans, who were shocked to discover (1) the concept of more than one "course" and (2) the lack of pizza as a staple entrée.

- **RENTING A VESPA:** Made popular by Gregory Peck and Audrey Hepburn in *Roman Holiday* (1953)—young tourist couples loved zooming through the piazza on their scooters, holding hands, being in love, not wearing helmets…eventually, perhaps, sharing a hospital room.

- **STAYING IN THE HOTEL:** As Arthur Frommer put it, there really was not much need to go past the hotel's Italian man—saturated outdoor café, especially given the cleanliness and stability of a Hilton Hotel. How do you say *hamburger* in Italian? Hilton.

OUTFITTING A HOTEL FOR A WORKDAY TRYST

KENNEDY'S BOOK OF SIGNATURE EXCUSES: A little-known follow-up to *Profiles in Courage*, the president offers iron-clad alibis like "at the dry cleaners," "walking the dog," and "in a Cabinet meeting." Your wife will never suspect a thing!

TELEVISION: Keep it off, for God's sake. In these troubled times there's no telling what cockamamie riot, war, assassination, or worse is going to come on and kill the mood.

FUZZY SLIPPERS: You're already treating yourself, why not go all the way?

EXTRA DUFFEL BAG: You're already paying for the hotel room and they have plenty of towels. They won't miss a few. Right?

CUMBERSOME GIFT FOR MISTRESS: Make sure it's bulky, expensive, and nonreturnable. Then she'll always have a little (big) piece of you to remind her of these special times.

SEND DOWN TO THE CONCIERGE FOR A HI-FI. Remember: East Coast jazz for before—get in the mood with Charlie Parker, Thelonious Monk, and Clifford Brown. West Coast jazz for after—cool down with a little Dave Brubeck.

KNEE BRACE: The secretaries get younger every year, but you're not some young buck. An ounce of prevention saves a pound of bills from your osteopath.

FRAMED HEADSHOT OF YOUR WIFE: For advanced philanderers only. Place on nightstand. At the moment between foreplay and intercourse, dramatically turn it toward the wall.

LIQUOR: Checking in without luggage looks suspicious. Kill two birds with one stone by lugging a Briefcase Liquor Cabinet™. Look professional coming in and going out. Contains more than eight kinds of fine alcohols.

RAINY-DAY ACTIVITIES

activities for
children

- **SEAT OLYMPICS**

  See which child can vault from the front seat to the back the fastest. Keeps them busy while you're driving around doing errands.

- **FANTASTIC PLASTIC BAGS**

  Why waste money on toys and books when an afternoon's fun comes free with every trip to the French cleaners. Now your little angels can be spacemen, space blobs, blob men, blob victims, pod men, bag pods, larvae, or a plastic bag that has attained sentience! These are just suggestions—let the imagination run wild! (The average child is shorter than a garment bag. You may want to pin it up a bit so they do not trip while running wild.)

- **SITTING IN FRONT OF THE TV**

  The downside of children using their imaginations is it can lead to a lot of cleanup on your part—one round of Cowboys and Indians, and the next thing you know your best cut-glass ashtray is on the floor in pieces! Thank goodness for television. Not only will they sit quietly but the stories will be historically accurate and your children's creativity won't be taxed.

- **PUT A NAME TO MOMMY'S SADNESS**

  A young child is an absolute sponge of observation, paying careful attention to things we adults take for granted. Save money on expensive trips to the analyst by harnessing your offspring's natural gifts.

- **CHOOSE BETWEEN MOMMY AND DADDY**

  Line up all your children by height. Describe a scenario in which either you or your husband dies (e.g., stroke, race riot, nuclear crisis). Have them choose who they would rather live with and why. Have them sign affidavits for use in later divorce proceedings.

- **HUCKLEBERRY GHOST**

  A plastic mask of a beloved cartoon character becomes a quiet commentary on the observed and the observer. Junior walks silently through your home, face obscured. It's like you're in a Bergman film!

- **PUNISHMENTS**

  Sometimes there can be too much fun. When fun gets away from you, it's time to lay down some punishments. Histrionics get a half day in the hole. Banish tantrums to the linen closet. Go make dinner. Remember to use the linen closet, not the pantry, in case you forget overnight; they'll have something to sleep on.

CUBAN MISSILE CRISIS!

The goofy game of Nuclear Brinkmanship

STart!

Use good ol' American coins for player pieces and go buy some dice. You want dice to be provided for you? What are you, a Communist?

CIA HEARS RUMORS

Cubans brag about their new "gifts" from Soviets.

Go forward 2 spaces

BAY OF PIGS DEBACLE 1961

The U.S. fails to overthrow Castro. Cuba worries about another invasion, and USSR decides to protect Cuba.

Go forward 2 spaces

U.S. MISSILES STATIONED IN TURKEY & ITALY

Pointing at the Soviets, making them nervous.

Go back 1 space

PRESIDENT MEETS WITH SOVIET FOREIGN MINISTER

Talk is cheap.

Lose a turn

SECRET LAUNCH SITES BUILT IN CUBA

USSR starts sending regiments to man the stations.

Go forward 1 space

MISSILES ARRIVE IN CUBA FROM USSR

Go back 2 spaces

DEFCON 2

Strategic Air Command raises security alert.

Go forward 2 spaces

U-2 SPY PHOTOS

Proof!

Go forward 6 spaces

OCTOBER 22

President makes TV and radio address publicly announcing knowledge of missile sites.

All players advance 1 space

EXCOMM ASSEMBLED

Roll again

October 14, 1962: A U-2 spy plane captures reconnaissance photos of a missile launch site deep in the forests of Cuba, complete with Soviet nuclear missiles! With Cuba only 90 miles from the U.S. coast, and with those Commie weapons' ballistic ranges of up to 2,800 miles, just a touch of the button by those dastardly Reds could wipe out every major American city except Seattle.

Help JFK and EXCOMM steer the situation safely—act fast, the future of the free world lies in the roll of your dice!

Safe

ARMAGEDDON
Go back to Start

STALEMATE
Neither side's going to budge.
Lose a turn

OPERATION "MONGOOSE" SUSPENDED
Put away those exploding cigars.
Lose a turn

U.S. BLOCKADE
Stops vessels from arriving in Cuba.
Go forward 1 space

SECRET NEGOTIATIONS
Roll again

ARMAGEDDON
Go back to Start

TURKEY BRISTLES
Prospect of losing NATO missiles.
Go back 3 spaces

OCTOBER 28
Khrushchev blinks. Announces on Radio Moscow intentions to withdraw nuclear missiles and stop work on Cuban launch sites.
Roll again

INVADE CUBA
Initiate World War III. Remove your player from the board; you lost.

SOVIET SHIPS ARE ON THEIR WAY!
Loaded with more missiles!
Lose a turn

PEACE!
EVERYBODY WINS!
The United States agrees not to invade Cuba and to schedule removal of medium-range ballistic missiles from Turkey. Soviets return Cuban nuclear warheads to USSR. A "hotline" is established between Washington, DC, and Moscow to prevent this kind of thing from happening again.

THE HANGED MAN.

Fun with Tarot

Invented by either ancient Egyptians or medieval Italian court seers—depending on who you ask—the Tarot card deck is both a game and a means of divination. Like a traditional playing card deck, the Tarot consists of four suits: wands, cups, swords, and pentacles. In addition to the four suits, known in Tarot as the minor arcana, the deck also has 22 trump cards, or major arcana. These consist of the more notorious Tarot cards: "Death," "The Lovers," "The Hanged Man," and so on. Each card holds a variety of esoteric meanings, which change based on how the divination is performed, which cards it's next to, the talent of the reader, the humidity in the air, and what you had for lunch.

But what do fin de siècle mystics and American mid-twentieth-century housewives have in common? The insatiable desire to know what men are up to, of course! So if there's a brooding, successful man in your life who tends to stare balefully into the distance, martini in hand, rather than tell you what's really on his mind, here's the perfect exercise to try on him once you can trick him into thinking he's sitting down for a new card game.

First, find a special container. Presentation is key. Think exotic-print scarf rather than Grandpa's cigar box. When shuffling the deck, squint your eyes or bite your lip. Remember to do a theatrical shuffle move, and twist some of the cards vertically, so there's a chance they will be played upside down. You may not feel like you're tapping into the cosmic ether yet, but function may follow your form if you fake it. While cutting the deck, have your subject ask what he wants to know. If he makes a pass at you here, feel free to end the reading. If this is a platonic relationship and your only role is to help the brooding man "find himself" while he is on a business trip to California, deal the cards in a diamond pattern. Right-side-up cards for your subject mean you can interpret the cards positively. So if, for example, the "Tower" card comes up, you could interpret it as your man's enemies burning in the hellish miasma of a cursed skyscraper. If the card is reversed, this is negative—maybe it's your subject who's doomed to fall from the heights.

Learning to read Tarot is a trial-and-error process. Don't worry about getting it right the first time. Making interpretations on your own takes practice, confidence, and a little knack for telling your man what you want him to hear—while making it sound like what he wants to hear.

THE FOOL.

STRENGTH.

MRS. **JOAN HARRIS**

based on costumes by janie bryant

Death Is
My Client

A Play in
One Act

by

Paul Kinsey

Dyna Moe is an illustrator and comedian.
She makes video shorts of minor renown.

In 2008, she became "Internet famous" for drawing a
scene every week of *Mad Men*'s second season.
She illustrated the very popular avatar maker "Mad Men Yourself"
for AMC in a similar style.
You probably already knew that.

She lives in New York City. This is her first book.

nobodyssweetheart.com